Weekend Cookery for Boys and Girls

Hello dear friends,

Welcome to Weekend Cookery !

Before you explore the book, you young aspiring little chefs, must read this letter that will explain how the book has been designed for your knowledge and benefit. Since you are going to be the main users of this book, you must know that it contains 52-step by step-easy to follow recipes with their illustrations along with 20 Quick Bites. For your benefits we have tried to give you the information about the dishes and the main ingredients used in the recipes along with their health benefits in short; if almost the same ingredients are repeated to create other recipes, information is not repeated. It is informed under which title that information will be available. So you must go through the recipes carefully before attempting any selected recipe. We have tried to mention origin of the recipes in short, too. Since the book also contains a few recipes for quick bites, you may use the ingredients or the raw material already available in your mom's kitchen. Most of the dishes will be cooked within 45 minutes to 1hour. We have recommended the use of Micro-oven (wherever possible) with a convection mode which is safe for children to use in comparison to the open fire flame. That doesn't mean that without a micro oven you are stuck. Gas flame, of course, can be used for cooking, and as such it is used for frying in some of the recipes.

But you must make a point to gather all the ingredients before cooking your selected item,. Moreover, all the ingredients, particularly the refrigerated ones should be at room temperature.

Even if you are already exposed to basic cooking, still our suggestion is that you must plan the cooking; select the dish/dishes; read the recipes carefully; collect all the raw material needed, and then go ahead confidently, so that you are better organized and have good time management. Proper planning always helps to work smoothly and efficiently Don't be shy to seek assistance from grownups around to understand the use of your cooking tools and to help you understand the cooking terminology and the ingredients properly. The lists are added in the book .Believe us, you will never go wrong

Utilize your holidays to experiment with food. Try the selected dishes in a group of friends or relatives, you will have more fun while cooking and later relishing your own creations.

Cooking is an art as well as a science. The knowledge of basics of any stream, art or science, is as important as learning the 3 Rs (when you just step in the field of education for the first time). To master the art as a hobby / profession, the knowledge of its methodology and technique are as essential. Later you can use your knowledge and creative instinct to innovate many more dishes, but only when your basics are clear.

In our workshops arranged with children like you, they get fully involved in the activities such as mixing and beating etc, and use their creativity for the presentation, too. Some photographs of our workshop are included in the book.

Have a wonderful time.

With Love,

Prabhjot Mundhir

Weekend Cookery for Boys and Girls

Acknowledgement

I would like to dedicate this book to all those children who love to experiment with food, to my grandchildren Amanat, Aaryaman, Rhea and to their peer groups. I am also grateful to all the children (and their parents) who come to attend my cookery workshops/classes from time to time. They all wanted children's cookbook with latest trendy recipes that are, not only, delicious and mouth watering, but also healthy; and are good for their growth. Interestingly, children do listen to the instructions of their teachers and instructors more than the parents, hence, this book with detailed instructions, step by step doable recipes and their illustrations.

Above all, I can't forget to thank my dear husband (now) Late Wing Commander. Mandhir Singh, for his unrelenting support at each stage developing this book. He was my best critic too. I would not have been what I am, had he not encouraged me to develop my hobby into a profession. His sudden demise delayed the publication of this book.

Prabhjot Mundhir

Index

Index

QUICK DISHES

Essentials

Cooks' Tools :

Children, in the absence of these useful items in the kitchen, it is almost impossible to produce good results regarding food dishes. Most of these items you will find in your mom's kitchen; **yet for** your own reference we are enlisting below these items, so that you can confirm before attempting to cook your favorite dishes.

You need:

Measuring cups : to measure flours or liquids

Measuring spoons : to measure baking powder/ soda, seasonings, spices

Scales : to weigh the flour, veggies, fruits etc.

Sieve : to sieve the flour and other dry ingredients

Strainer : to strain the liquids

Trove : an open vessel to collect sieved items or to mix dough

Rolling pin : to roll the pastry/ chapatti etc

Tin cutter/opener : to open the cans

A pair of scissors : to cut the various things

Wooden spoons : to mix the cake batter or cook in the non-stick pans

Chopping board : to chop / cut fruits and vegetables

Knives : to cut and chop fruits, pastry, veggies etc

Palate Knife : for spreading butter / cheese / chutney, icing etc

Grater : to grate cheese, chocolate or veggies for use

Pastry cutters/ Biscuit cutter : to cut the cookies and biscuits etc.

Mixing bowls : to mix the ingredients for cooking

Baking trays : for baking cakes and pastries

Muffin tray : for baking muffins and cup cakes

Assorted cake tins : cake tins of various sizes and shapes

Spatula : flat rubber spoon to remove the dough from the bowls

Electric beater/ Wire whisker : to beat/whisk eggs or cream

Electric mixer/ Food processor : to liquidize or to puree veggies/fruits

Lemon squeezer : to squeeze the juice from the lemons

Pans & Saucepans : to cook eggs or to steam veggies or make sauce

Griddle/ Tava : to make chapatti/ paratha etc.

Oven gloves : to remove the dishes / plates /baking trays from hot oven

Apron : to be worn over your clothes to avoid staining/dirtying

Kitchen towels : to be used for cleaning / sweeping working surface

Steaming basket : to steam the vegetables, fish and meats etc.

Cooks' Terminology

It consists of those special words in the dictionary of cooking that are regularly used in the recipes to explain the action to be taken by the cooks, such as Stirring, Baking, Mixing, Sieving etc. Given below is the list of the terminology in the alphabetical order.

You need:

Bake : Cook food in the oven

Baste : Brush the food with pan juices, especially when the food is being grilled /roasted to improve the flavour

Beat : Use a whisk/wooden spoon to mix the ingredients vigorously

Boil : Cook food in boiling water. When water reaches the boiling point and bubbles appear on the surface that means water is ready to cook food

Cream : Beat ingredients together, such as butter, sugar or egg whites, until light and fluffy for cakes and cookies etc

Fry : Cook food in hot oil

Garnish : Decorate food with fresh herbs, vegetables, sliced fruits or chocolates etc to make the food look aesthetically appealing

Grease : Use a pastry brush to grease the baking tins/trays with melted butter or vegetable oil to stop food from sticking

Knead : Mix dry and wet ingredients with the fingers to gather them in a mass and then push and press the mixture with palms, stretch it if needed and knead again till the dough is smooth, elastic and pliable.

Note : You can also knead the ingredients in the dough maker of a food processor

Mash : Squash everything with a potato masher, fork or your hands until smooth, especially boiled potatoes or vegetables

Pinch : You may find this term in some recipes, eg, pinch the sides of a pastry or sprinkle a pinch of spices on a dish etc. That means as much as you can hold with your index finger and thumb together

Season : Add extra flavor to food using salt, pepper, herbs and spices

Sieve : Shake flour, coco powder or icing sugar salt etc. through a sieve to make it light or get lumps out of icing sugar or coco powder

Simmer : Cook a liquid over a low fire/ gentle heat, so that the surface does not boil

Stir : Mix the food lightly with a spatula / wooden spoon while the food is being cooked for even cooking

Whisk : Beat wet ingredients with a wire whisk or electric whisk to make them light and fluffy such as eggs or cream

Weights and Measures

Approximate Conversion Guide

- 1 tablespoon (tbsp) : 15 ml/gm
  =3 tsp
- 1 tea spoon (tsp) : 5 ml/gm
  =3 tsps make 1 tbsp
- 1 cup : 240 ml/gm
  =16 tbsp

Approximate Conversion Guide

- 1/2 Cup : 20 ml/gm
  =8 tsp
- 1/3 Cup : 75 to 80 ml/gm
  =5 to 5½ tbsp
- 1/4 Cup : 60 ml/gm
  =4 tbsp

11 Important Dos and Don'ts:

- To be safe and systematic while working in the kitchen.
- Wash your hands before you begin work in the kitchen and after handling meats.
- Wear an apron and roll your sleeves up to keep your clothes clean.
- Tie your hair if it is very long
- Collect together all the ingredients that you need for selected dish before you start cooking. Measure and weigh them.
- Always have an adult's help when in the kitchen.
- Always use oven gloves when handling hot food.
- Always preheat the oven before baking.
- Be very careful with sharp knives.
- Pan's and saucepan's handles should be kept on the side to avoid any accident.
- Don't open the oven door while something is cooking inside, especially cakes. Cakes can easily spoil when rising. If curious, you may peep in from safe distance.

Glossary: Important English words and their Hindi names

Hindi	English
Aaloo	Potato
Mango	Aam
Adrak	Ginger
Ajwain	Carom Seeds
Akhrot	Walnuts
Anaar	Pomegranate
Ananas	Pineapple
Angoor	Grapes
Amchur	Mango powder
Amla	Gooseberry
Badam	Almonds
Badi Ilaichi	Black Cardamoms
Baking Powder	Baking powder
Besan	Bengal Gram flour
Bhindi	Lady Fingers/Okra
Bhutta	Corn
Chai	Tea
Chapati	Flat griddle-roasted Wheat circlet

Hindi	English
Chaat	Combination of Food items Chutneys, spices
Chaat Masala	Powdered Spices used for Chaat
Chhote Aaloo	Baby Potatoes
ChhoteTamatar	Cherry Tomatoes
Chhoti ilaichi	Green Cardamoms
Chukander	Beetroot
Chutney	Spicy sauce
Dahi	Curd
Desi Ghee	Clarified Butter
Dhania	Coriander
Dalchini	Cinnamon Sticks
Doodh	Milk
Falooda	Cornflour noodles
France Bean	French Beans
Gajar	Carrot
Genhu	Wheat

Hindi	English
Gobi	Cauliflower
Gur/Gud	Jaggery/Coarse Brown Sugar
Haldi	Turmeric
Hulwa	Semi solid Sweet Confection
Hara Dhania	Coriander leaves
Hara Pyaj	Spring Onions
HariMirchi	Green Chilli
Hari Gobi	Broccoli
Hari Chutney	Spicy sauce made of Coriander and Mint
Heeng	Asafetida/Asafoetida
Imli	Tamarind
Imli Chutney/Saunth	Spicy sauce made of Tamarind pulp
Jeera	Cumin seeds
Kabab	Roasted pieces of Vegetables, and Meats
Kabuli Chana	Chick Peas/white chana
KadiPatta	Curry leaves
Kaju	Cashew Nuts

Hindi	English
Kala Namak	Rock Salt
Kala Chana	Bengal Gram
Kali Mirch (Kali Miri)	Black Pepper
Karela	Bitter Gourd
Kela	Banana
Keema	Minced Meat
Kishmish	Raisins
Khumb	Mushrooms
LalMirch	Red Chilli
Lassi	Butter milk / A drink made of Curd
Lehsun	Garlic
Machhi	Fish
Madhu/Shahad	Honey
Makhan	Butter
Makki	Maize
Malai	Fresh Cream
Maida	Refined Flour / White Flour
Mutter	Green Peas
Maash/Urad	Black Gram
Muli	Radish

Hindi	English
Murgi	Chicken
Moong	Green Gram whole
Namak	Salt
Moong Dhuli	Green Gram split, skinless
Mungphali	Peanuts/Groundnuts
Nariyal	Coconut
Nashpati	Pears
Nimbu	Lemon
Palak	Spinach
Paneer	Cottage Cheese
Paneer Ka Pani	Whey
Papita	Papaya
Phal	Fruits
Phulka/Roti	Dry puffed Wheat Circlet
Pilav/Pulao	Meat or Vegetables Rice Dish
Pista	Pistachio Nuts
Paratha	Layered griddle fried Roti
Pudina	Mint leaves
Puri	Crisp Deep fried Wheat Circlet

Hindi	English
Pyaaj	Onions
Raie	Mustard Seeds
Rajma	Kidney Beans
Rava/Suji	Semolina
Sev	Apple
Sepreta Doodh	Toned Milk
Sirka	Vinegar
Sukha Meva	Dry Fruits
Soya Paneer	Tofu
Tamatar	Tomato
Tamatar Pulp	Tomato Puree
Tandoori	Any food cooked in Tandoor
Tarkari	Vegetables
Tel	Oil or cooking oil
Til	Sesame Seeds
Tulsi	Basil
Urad dal	Black Gram

Delicious Chocolate Muffins

Ingredients :

- *1 and 1/2 Cup -Flour*
- *1 cup - Sugar*
- *150 gm - Butter*
- *1 large - Egg*
- *1/2 cup - Coco powder*
- *1/2 cup or 2 tbsp more - Milk lukewarm*
- *1 tsp l/2cup - Baking Soda*
- *1 tsp - Baking powder*
- *1/2 Cup - Walnuts (opt)*
- *12 - Paper cups or Muffin tin for 12*

Note:

Though here we are preparing the muffins, but with the same recipe you can bake a chocolate cake. Here step by step photographs are given to understand the process of making any cake.

Preparation and Cooking:

- Lightly **brush** muffin tin tray / cake cups with **butter or cooking oil.**
- **Sieve** together flour, cocoa, baking powder and baking soda twice.
- Coarsely **grind** walnuts.
- **Mix** sugar and butter together. **Beat** with a hand beater or electric hand beater till well mixed, light, fluffy and creamy. Add egg and beat again nicely.

Chocolate Muffins

*One of the most precious gifts of **Mexico** to the world is **Chocolate.** In its simplest and ancient form chocolate was used to make a drink by boiling cocoa beans in water, and after adding sugar it was served as an invigorating and restorative beverage. Now it is used extensively in cooking to bake a variety of cakes and to make candies, delicious desserts and beverages etc.*

To be continued

Note: Powder sugar in a dry grinder after measuring it if the sugar crystals are bigger.

- **Add** milk to the creamy mixture and **beat** once until well blended.
- Now **add** flour mixture spoon by spoon and keep mixing properly.
- **Put** 2 tbsp cake batter in each cavity of muffin tin or paper cups.
- **Preheat CONVECTION** mode of your microwave oven for 3 minutes, or your electric oven / oven of a cooking range to 190 degrees Celsius for 10 minutes.
- **Wear gloves** and **place** the tray on high rack in the preheated oven. **Set** the time and **bake** for 17 minutes on 190 degrees Celsius. Stand them for 5 minutes in the oven.
- **Remove** the muffins and **cool**. Use tip of a palate knife/butter knife to remove cakes.

Step 1

Caution/Advise: You may take an adult's help to take out the muffin tray from the hot oven.

Serving: Serve the yummy muffins at room temperature with a **beverage** or as such in between the meals. Sometimes carry in your **lunch box** when favourite snack is allowed.

Step 2

Important: For the best results, all the ingredients such as butter, eggs, milk and cream etc used for cakes, cookies and other dishes, should always be at room temperature.

Do you know? Chocolate is nutritious. It boosts your energy, elevates your mood and releases stress. But eat chocolates or Coco based goodies as a treat because, too, much of anything is bad for you.

Interesting fact: *The **source** of chocolate is **Cocoa** beans. Beans are picked up, opened, dried in the sun and then are sent to the factory. There they are cleaned, roasted and ground to a thick sticky paste. Finally sugar is mixed in to make the paste sweet; after a lot of more work to make it smooth, chocolate is moulded into blocks; and finally converted into either chips or bite sized pieces, or even small bars to melt in your mouth.*

Step 3

Cooking time: 20 minutes.

Potato Cheese Balls

Ingredients :

- *300gm - Boiled potatoes*
- *1/4 cup - Soft breadcrumbs*
- *1/2 cup - Cheese grated*
- *1/2 tsp - pepper powder*
- *1 tsp - Mint powdered*
- *Salt to taste*
- *12 - cloves*

Preparation and Cooking:

- **Brush** a baking tray with a little cooking oil.
- **Grate** potatoes. **Mix** breadcrumbs, half the cheese, salt, pepper and mint with potatoes; **knead** well to pliable dough; **divide** it into equal portions, **roll** and flatten;(shape each portion like a fish and stick 1 clove as its eye, if you like.)
- **Spread** remaining cheese in a plate and lightly **coat** top portion of the fish with cheese; and place in the baking tray.
- **Preheat** CONVECTION mode of your microwave for 3 minutes to 180 degrees Celsius. Or bake them in a preheated electric oven or gas cooking range.
- **Wear gloves** and **place** the tray in the oven. **Bake** for 20 minutes.
- Wear gloves and **remove** the tray. **Cool**. With the tip of a palate knife remove them carefully.
- **Caution/Advise:** You may take an adult's help to remove the tray from the hot oven.

Serving: Serve at room temperature with **Tomato sauce or Green chutney.** Take in a lunch box to school if you like.

Potato Cheese Balls

This innovative dish made of potatoes and cheese gives the good nutrition to the body.

*Little chefs, do you know that potatoes and cheese provide **Carbohydrates and Protein** to your body which, particularly, you the growing children need them more to build healthy body and sound mind. Carbohydrate in potatoes fills your tummy and gives you the energy to keep going; and the **Protein in Cheese** (a milk product) builds your body and helps you grow those extra inches.*

Refreshing Orange Ice

Orange Ice

Ingredients :

- *2 cups-Orange juice*
- *1/2 cup-Sugar*
- *1 and 1/2 cup-Water*
- *Lemon rind-From 1 lemon (optional)*
- *1-Freezer tray /Ice cream tray and a few Orange segments for garnishing*

Preparation and Cooking:

- **Chill** a freezer/ice cream tray.
- **Grate** uncut lemon lightly from all sides to collect lemon rind.
- **Place** sugar and water in a micro-safe jug and **Boil** it for 5 minutes on HIGH i.e. 100% power and stand it for 5 minutes; remove and **Stir**, so that sugar is fully dissolved. **Cool.**
- **Strain** through a sieve and mix orange juice with it. **Add** lemon rind and mix. **Pour** in the chilled tray carefully and **Deep freeze** for 3 to 4 hours till slushy or half set.
- **Remove** the tray from the freezer and with a fork or a hand beater **Mix** it nicely and freeze again for 4 to 5 hours till hard.

Serving:

Remove the tray and **Soften** the orange ice for 10 minutes. **Break** with a fork and **Pile up** in 4 small stemmed glasses. Quickly decorate with orange segments and serve as a cool treat.

*Mexican orange ice, prepared with fresh or preserved juice and sugar, lip smacking water ice is very soothing in hot summer months. It is made like **Italian Granita** that is served after any heavy meal.*

To be continued

Variation:

Use well flavoured Lemonade instead of orange juice and make Lemon ice. Mix Water melon juice, sugar and lemon juice to get Water melon Ice. You may even use Mango juice to make Mango ice.

Watermelon Ice

Healthy facts:

Orange is a citrus fruit. Orange juice is full of Vitamin C that keeps the gums healthy; and Sugar in this cold soothing dish gives necessary energy to the body; by replenishing the water content in the body and removes the fatigue.

Do you know?

Exquisite 'Mexicans fruit Sorbets and Ices' are very popular throughout Mexico, and different regions have developed their own recipes according to the availability of local seasonal fruits. These delicately flavoured ices of fresh fruits are very refreshing 'frozen desserts'.

Mango Ice

Awesome Apple Tarts

Apple Tarts

Ingredients :

For Tarts:

- *1 and 1/2 cup - Flour*
- *1/2 cup - Butter*
- *5 tbsp - Chilled water*
- *1/4 tsp - Salt.*
- *3 Apples*
- *1/4 cup - Sugar*
- *1 tsp - Lemon juice*
- *1/4 tsp - Cinnamon powder*
- *1tbsp - Chopped dry-fruit for garnishing.*

Preparation and Cooking:

- **Sieve** flour and salt together; **mix butter** with your **finger tips** till the mixture **resembles breadcrumbs; add** water and make dough. If required, sprinkle a few more drops of cold water **to hold** the ingredients together. **Knead** it well to pliable dough. **In summers wrap it in cling film and refrigerate for 20 minutes before rolling.**
- **Take** it out; **divide** in 2 parts and **Roll out** one part of dough on lightly loured surface. Tarts should be about **1/8-inch in thickness. Cut** 8 circles of almost 3-inch in diameter using a cutter / Katori or a bottle cap and **fit** in the tart shells, **trimming extra** dough. Place them in a baking tray.
- **Preheat** the **CONVECTION** mode for 3 minutes. **Wear the gloves and place** them on **high rack** of your oven. **Bake** for 15 minutes on 180 degrees Celsius. **Stand** them inside the oven for 5 minutes.
- Or **bake** them in preheated electric oven or oven of cooking range for 20 minutes. Stand them for 5 minutes in the oven.
- **Wear gloves** and **remove** the tray. **Cool.**

  Advise: You may take an adult's help to remove the tray from the hot oven. This recipe will give you **16** tarts.

*All time favourite **'Apple tarts'** are made of butter, flour and apples. The term 'tart' is used in England and France, but in America, the same dish is called 'single crusted pie'. The tarts, not only satisfy the sweet tooth but also give you lots of energy.*

To be continued

- **Remove** the shells and **cool**. Take them out carefully with the tip of a palate knife carefully.
- **Repeat the process with other half of dough**, and **bake the same way.**
- **Peel and cut apples** in the small pieces and **sprinkle lemon juice** to avoid de-colouration. In a micro-safe bowl, **combine** all the ingredients of apple filling; **mix well** and **Cook** for 4 minutes, stirring every 1 minute.
- **Take** out the filling. **Mash the cooked apples** with a wooden spoon, **add** cinnamon powder, **stir** and **cool it** completely.
- **Fill the baked tart shells** with the filling and decorate the tarts with dry fruit.

Serving: Serve the tarts as a snack.

Tips: *You can fill up the tarts with any melted lemon filling, melted jam / melted chocolate also. You may even fill them up with any savoury mixture and serve as a starter.*

Health notes: *It is said, 'An apple a day, keeps the doctor away', yes, true, because apple is a fruit which contains soluble fiber that reduces cholesterol; it fills the tummy; and it also contains flavonoids that prevent heart ailments, stroke and chances of having cancer.*

And to you children*, this tasty dish gives you all the goodness of applesand butter. The fibers in the apples help in your digestive system and consequently, it works smoothly.Butter, a nutrienthas fat that helps you to absorb some of the vitamins from the other foods you eat, so that the digestive system runs smoothly.*

Variation: *Orange tarts/ Lemon tarts / Chocolate tarts etc.*

Cooking time: 30 minutes and preparation time extra.

Step by step - Apple tarts

Step - 1

Step - 2

Step -3

Step - 4

Step - 5

Lemon Tarts

Mischievous Cheese Coins

Ingredients :

- *12 slices - White/brown bread*
- *1 and ½ cup - Paneer / cottage cheese*
- *1medium - Boiled potato*
- *1 tbsp - Flour*
- *2 tsp - White pepper powder*
- *1/2 tsp - Mint powder*
- *1/4 cup - Grated cheese*
- *Salt to taste*

Garnishing:

- *24-Black peppercorns.*
- *1/4 cup - Grated cheese*
- *1/4 - Red pepper*

Preparation and Cooking:

- With the help of a **cookie cutter** or small katori, **cut** the roundels out of bread slices.
- **Place** the remaining portions of bread slices in electric grinder and make fresh breadcrumbs.
- **Cut** the red pepper into **12 thin strips** of 3/4th-inch long pieces.
- In a trove **mix togethe**r grated potato, paneer, soft breadcrumbs, cheese, flour, mint, salt and pepper powder. Knead the mixture to fine dough. **Divide** dough into 12 equal portions.
- **Sprea**d 1 portion of dough on 1 roundel of bread. **Place** 2 peppercorns as eyes and 1 small strip of **red pepper** like a mouth. Finish making all the roundels this way and place them in a baking tray.
- **Preheat** the **CONVECTION** mode of your microwave to 180 degrees Celsius for 3 minutes. Bake cheese roundels in hot oven for 12 minutes.

Mischievous Cheese Coins

***Cheese** is a product of curds, drained and, most often than not, fermented. Every country has its own special cheese. For example, Gruyere from Switzerland, Cheddar from England, Parmesan and Gorgonzola from Italy and Gouda from Holland are a few names. It is believed that no other country has so great variety and range of cheese as France. In India, though 'Paneer' (cottage cheese) is more popular since Vedic period, but now many Indian companies produce good variety of tasty and tingly cheese that suits our taste*

To be continued

- **Or** bake them in a preheated electric oven / cooking range for 15 minutes.
- Remove the tray.

Serving:

Serve this innovative dish of crisp roundels at room temperature with or without **Tomato sauce** as an evening snack.

Important:

Do you know that Paneer / Cheese, a milk product has good quality **high protein and calcium** too. Protein is the most important nutrient needed by human body, as it repairs and rebuilds cells that restore our health; and Calcium is an important mineral that helps make the **teeth and bones** inside the body **strong.** It contains all the essential amino acids which feed our brain and the nervous system. It is rich in **Vitamin A, B, and E.** Vegetarians can get enough **Vitamin B-12** essential for everyone. **Moreover, it is a good protein for stomach.**

And the **bread** (base of the coins), a wheat product is a **Carbohydrate** food which gives you **long lasting energy** to run and play without getting tired right away.

Enjoy the crisp cheese coins with friends or siblings.

Cooking time: 15 minutes.

Strawberry Mousse

Strawberry Mousse

*The **strawberry** is called **'the queen of fruits'** in Asian countries as it is packed with health benefits. In comparison to so many other fruits (such as apples, bananas or oranges) strawberries have the highest amount of nutrients. Some people consider them a **'power food'.** "Strawberries are the angels of the earth, innocent and sweet with green leafy wings reaching heaven ward". These delicious berries not only just please our palates, but also are packed with a **'healthy punch'.** The potassium, vitamin K and magnesium in strawberry are important for **bone health.** Vitamin C in it is an effective antioxidant that helps in lowering blood pressure. The **dietry fiber** in strawberry helps to keep digestion regular as well as **curbs overeating.** It is low in calories and high in fiber.*

Ingredients :

- *20 no - Strawberries*
- *1/2 cup - Milk*
- *1 and 1/2 cups - Mascarpone cheese*
- *Or home-made soft cheese (paneer)*
- *1/2 cup - Strawberry sauce / crush*
- *1 and 1/4 tbsp - Gelatin*

Note: it is important that all the ingredients are at room temperature. If **Cheese** and **Strawberries** are stored under refrigeration, take them out at least 2 hours before use

Preparation and Cooking:

- **Grease** lightly 4 to 6 small glass bowls; **rinse** under tap water without touching inside and **place** them in deep freezer to be chilled.
- **Clean and chop**16 strawberries and **save** the remaining 4 for garnishing.
- **Place** chopped strawberries, soft cheese, strawberry crush and milk in an electric blender and **churn** to mix.
- **Mix** gelatin with 3 tbsp water in a small bowl and **dissolve** it over

To be continued

a pan of hot water until all the crystals are fully dissolved. **Pour** it in the blender and **churn** the mixture once again.

- **Remove** the chilled bowls from the freezer and **pour** the strawberry mixture in them. **Place** the bowls once again in the freezer compartment for 1 hour. Then **remove** and **store** under refrigeration till to be used.

Serving:

Slice the remaining strawberries and **garnish** the individual bowls artistically and **serve** cold.

Tips:

Chilling the moulds before-hand reduces the setting time to half.

Preparation time: 20 minutes for preparation and chilling time extra.

Fresh Strawberries

Colourful Dollops Cake

Ingredients :

- *1 and 1/2 - cup Flour*
- *100-gm Butter*
- *3/4-cup Sugar*
- *1/2 - cup Milk*
- *3 - Eggs*
- *1and1/4tsp Baking powder*
- *A few drops of Edible Food colours such as Red Green and Yellow each*

For Butter Icing (opt): 100 gm Butter, Icing sugar and any colour of your choice.

Colourful Dollops Cake

Preparation and Cooking:

- **Prepare** a cake mould. Line it with butter paper or brown paper and brush it with a little melted butter. Keep it aside.
- **Sieve** flour and baking powder twice.
- **Cream** butter and sugar together with an electric hand beater.
- **Add** eggs one by one and **mix** till the mixture is smooth.
- **Add** dry ingredients and milk to **butter mixture** alternately. **Put 2 tbsp** sieved flour and mix, now **add** a little milk and mix. Thus consume all the flour and milk. **Beat** the cake batter once again and **divide** it into three parts.
- **Preheat** the oven to 190 degrees Celsius.
- **Colour** each part with a separate colour, eg. one part with **red**,

Step 1

Step 2

Step 3

Step 4

To be continued

second with **green** and **third** with yellow colour.

- Now **start adding** all the three parts of cake batter **spoon by spoon** alternately in the baking dish.
- **Bake** this colourful cake in the hot oven for 35 to 40 minutes. **Check** the cake by inserting the cake needle in the center of the cake and it should come out dry. **Remove** the cake from the oven.

  Note: If by chance the needle is a little **sticky, place** the cake again in hot oven and **bake** further for next 5 minutes **switch off Leave** the cake in the oven for 10 minutes and then remove it. **Cool** it for 15 minutes on the kitchen platform and **invert** on the cooling rack. Let it cool properly. **Remove** the butter paper carefully and **transfer** the cake to a serving plate. Cut into pieces and serve it if not using icing.

- **Prepare icing** by mixing butter and icing sugar together. **Add** the colour chosen for icing and **beat** it till smooth. With the help of an adult **cut the cake from the center** and with a palate knife **apply** the icing thinly on one part. **Place** the other part of the cake on top and **cover** it with icing. **Decorate** it as you like.

Serving:

Cut the cake into squares and serve. You can see the colourful effect in each piece. Enjoy it.

Baking time: 40 minutes.

Step 5

Step 6

Step 7

Step 8

Noodle Salad with Chinese Dressing

Noodle Salad with Chinese Dressing

Ingredients :

- *200 gm - Instant noodles*
- *2 - Carrots*
- *1 - Green pepper*
- *8 to 10 leaves - Cabbage*
- *3 to 4 - Spring onions*

For Dressing: Combine in a bottle 3 tbsp - Table vinegar, 1 tbsp - Soy sauce, 2 tbsp - Olive oil/ sesame oil, 1 tbsp - Chili-Garlic sauce, 1/4 tsp - Pepper powder, Salt to taste if needed be.(Soy sauce is very salty, so check the salt before adding it to salad). Shake well and keep aside.

Preparation and Cooking:

- **Peel** carrots and **clean** capsicum and **cut in juliennes** (veggies cut in thin match stick style strips). **Shred** cabbage. Clean and cut spring onions.
- **Steam** carrots for 2 minutes in the steaming basket of a microwave oven. Remove and **mix** with the other vegetables. Cover for 3 minutes.
- **Boil** 6 cups water with 1 tsp salt and 2 tsp oil in a large pan on high fire, add noodles and cook till soft but still crisp.
- **Mix** noodles and vegetables in a bowl; pour the salad dressing over it and stir with a fork. Check the salt. Cover the bowl and cool for 30 minutes under refrigeration before serving.

Serving: Serve it as a salad or even as a meal.

Cooking: 35 minutes.

__Noodles__ the staple food of Chinese, has become a popular meal among other Asian countries as well as in many western countries. According to a report published by the __World Instant Noodles Association,__ India stands fourth in the global instant noodles consumption. Noodles are one of the most versatile pasta that can be prepared soft boiled, stir-fried, crisp fried and even soupy.

In this simple recipe we are using the boiled noodles to prepare a salad with Chinese dressing.

Delicious-Creamy Home-made Yogurt (Dahi)

Ingredients :

- *500 ml - Boiled milk cooled to lukewarm state*
- *1 tbsp - Yogurt to be used as starter*
- *A bowl with a lid.*

Preparation and Cooking:

- **Mix starter** with ¼ cup of milk nicely and **add** it to the lukewarm milk. **Stir** well and **pour** into the bowl with a lid.
- **Place** it in a warm place to **incubate** for 6 to 8 hours or **stand** it **overnight.**

  Note: You may set it in an oven with its light on / place it in a casserole / or in a hot case with the lid on, so that it gets the right temperature to set properly.
- After the yogurt is set, **place** it in the refrigerator just to **prevent** / avoid yogurt from becoming **sour.** Eat it either for breakfast or lunch along with Roti / Paratha / Rice or Pulao etc. It's a good source of Probiotic Food.

Tips:

- *For proper fermentation yogurt needs the temperature of 110 degrees Celsius.*
- *Avoid adding starter to very hot or cold milk, the hot milk will curdle and cold will not set it properly.*
- *You may set yogurt in individual portions. For this after mixing starter to the milk, pour it into 4 small glass bowls or glasses kept in a tray. Cover and place tray in a warm place.*

Home - made Yogurt (Dahi)

Plain un-flavoured yogurt *is an ancient food and is well known for being a healthy food. Our body needs a healthy amount of 'good bacteria' in the digestive tract and most of the yogurts are made using active good bacteria. It is nutritious. The Yogurt that is made at home is healthier, fresher and less tart to taste. In India, home-made yogurt is called CURDS in English and DAHI in Hindi. In most parts of India fresh home-made yogurt is an integral part of daily meals.*

To be continued

Variations:
Flavoured Yogurts:

- **After boiling** full cream milk, immediately **add ¼ cup sugar** and stir to mix. **Cool**. Then **add** 1 tsp vanilla essence/, almond essence, peppermint/coffee powder/ cocoa powder/cinnamon powder or ginger powder etc.
- **Instead** of sugar, you may add **¼ cup honey** /maple syrup or chocolate syrup along with **2 tbsp dry milk powder** to the lukewarm milk and follow the process of setting it. After **adding powder milk, mix it thoroughly to avoid any lumps.**

Preparation time: 15 minutes and setting time 6 to 8 hours.

Health Benefits:

*Yogurt being one of the dairy products has all the **goodness** of milk. It is a good source of **Protein, Calcium, Phosphorus, Potassium, Riboflavin and Vitamin B-12.** It has healing properties. Individuals who suffer from **Lactose intolerance**, it is easier for them to digest yogurt because enzymes from yogurt bacteria break down the lactose during its fermentation process.*

Crostini

Crostini

Ingredients :

- *6 slices - Day old bread,*
- *½ no - Roasted red pepper*
- *6 no - Cheese slices or thinly sliced Cheddar cheese*
- *Pepper - to taste.*

Preparation and Cooking:

- **Cut the bread slices** into any shape of your choice. It may be circle, triangle, oval, heart shape or a star.
- **Preheat** the oven to 190 degrees Celsius.
- **Cut cheese slices** also in the same shape.
- **Place** a cut slice of cheese on the bread.
- **Cut small** roundels of pepper too. You may cut any other fancy shape and place on top of the cheese.
- **Sprinkle** a little pepper on top of each piece.
- **Place in the** greased baking tray and bake for **10 minutes** or till cheese melts.

Serving:

Serve Crostini **hot** from the oven or serve it at **room** temperature.

***Crostini,** the small pieces of toasted bread are made with various toppings and are served as one of the **Italian antipasti** / starter with hot or cold drinks. These different shaped crisp bites are excellent accompaniment to soups also. They can be topped with cheese, seafood or meats.*

To be continued

Note:

If you increase the number of bread slices, **increase** the quantity of cheese also.

Tips:

If you are using cheese slices, after cutting the required number of shapes from them, the trimmings can be used either in baking, in cheese sauce or while cooking omelets.

What is so good about Bread and Cheese?

*Bread is a **carbohydrate** food and it gives you long lasting **energy**. Carbohydrate also gives you **fiber** which helps your **digestive system** work smoothly. **Cheese** that is made of milk contains Calcium. Calcium is an important mineral that helps **make the bones** inside your body **strong.** It also keeps your **teeth** strong.*

Cooking time: 20 minutes.

Homemade Chocolates

Ingredients :

- *Chocolate compound of your choice - Light / Dark compound or White compound*
- *Chocolate crackles (opt)*
- *Nuts (opt)*
- *Chocolate moulds of any shape.*

Preparation and Cooking:

- **Choose** the chocolate of your choice to be used. Any of the compounds / chocolate chips or any solid chocolate bar will do.
- **Melt the chocolate. Break** the selected chocolate bar into pieces and **place** it in a micro-safe bowl and **cook** on micro HIGH for 30 seconds. **Take out** the bowl and **stir** chocolate mixture. Cook again for 30 seconds and stir; **repeat** the cooking process till the chocolates is completely melted. **Do not overcook.**
- **Add** a few drops of peppermint extract if you like the flavour.
- **Pour** the melted chocolate into the moulds. When the chocolate is still hot, **fill** the moulds. Fill the moulds to their rims. If necessary use the **back of the spoon** to smoothen chocolate into the corners. To help the chocolate **settle** properly in the moulds **tap** the mold lightly on the working surface/counter. This action

Homemade Chocolates

*It will be interesting to know **how chocolate is made.** It is made of beans that grow in pods on a **cocoa tree.** The pods are picked up from the tree; cut open and scooped out; spread out and left to dry in the sun. The dried beans are taken to a factory where they are cleaned, roasted and ground to a thick sticky paste. Then sugar is mixed in so the paste becomes sweeter. Since it is still gritty, it is squeezed, stirred, melted and cooled. Finally the chocolate is moulded into blocks; then either cut into portions and packed or made into little chips that are used in making biscuits, cakes and cookies etc.*

To be continued

Strawberry Jelly with Mango pulp

Ingredients :

- *100 gm - Strawberry Jelly crystals*
- *500 ml / 2 and 1/2 cup - Water*
- *1 and 1/2 cup - Mango pulp*
- *2 tbsp - Sugar (opt)*
- *1/4 cup - Milk*
- *1/4 cup - Fresh cream*
- *1 tbsp - Gelatin*
- *6 small - Strawberries / a few Mango pieces*
- *6 - Ice cream cups.*

Strawberry Jelly with Mango pulp

Preparation and Cooking:

- **Place** mango pulp, sugar, milk and cream in a blender; **blend** to smooth mixture and take out in a bowl.
- **Mix** gelatin with 4 tbsp water and **dissolve** on the bowl of hot water. **Mix** it with mango pulp. **Fill** the ice cream cups up to half and place under freezer.
- **Mix** strawberry jelly with water in a micro-safe bowl and **cook** on for 8 minutes on 100% power that is HIGH. **Take out** crystal clear jelly from the microwave when **cool.**
  You may cook jelly on gas heat also.
- **Take out** the ice cream cups from the freezer and **pour** jelly over mango pulp; once again **place** cups under freezer for 30 minutes. Remove and keep the cups under refrigeration till required to be served.

Mango *- the king of fruits, as you know, is a summer fruit. Not only it is delicious but also supplies contents to digestive system. Its consumption alkalizes the whole body. Along with improving our digestive system, it also lowers cholesterol, clears skin and improves eye health. Research says that antioxidant compounds in mango protect against colon, breast and prostrate cancer. They say it helps in diabetes too.*
Any dish prepared with mango enhances the taste of even ordinary dish.

To be continued

removes the air bubbles and smoothen the chocolates. At this stage you may add chocolate crackers or nuts etc.

- Let the chocolates **cool**. Leave them on the counter to harden or place them in a refrigerator for 30 minutes or so. Do not try to **unmould** until completely cool.
- **Remove** the chocolates from the moulds carefully. Eat them right away or wrap them in chocolate wrapper and store.

Serving:

Serve them anytime after the meals or during festival season. Or pack them in an attractive small bag and gift to the dear ones.

Tips:

You can make your own chocolate Lolly-pops. For this you have to have Lolly-pop chocolate mould.

Important:

Do not forget to brush your teeth after consuming chocolates of your choice, so that you keep them healthy.

Cooking time: Depends on the quantity you are preparing.

Serving:

Garnish with fresh strawberries or mangoes and serve cold.

Note:

Always add gelatin to a mixture at room temperature or to a warm product. If added to cold mixture, it will form either lumps or strings.

Preparation time: 20 minutes. Chilling time extra

Health Benefits of eating Jelly:

Despite being sweet, jelly has many nutritional benefits for the body. First of all it improves Gut health system; protects joints and lowers joint pain; improves skin quality; maintains heart; makes the bones stronger and gelatin in jelly boosts our immune system. In short by eating jelly our mood is elevated. It has no fat, so a cup of jelly or jelly and fruit can be easily consumed often.

A child's happiness after enjoying eating Jelly

Pizza/Pitza

Zucchini Pizza

Ingredients :

- *1 cup - Cooked chicken shredded*
- *1/2 cup - Pineapple chopped*
- *12 - Baby corns halved lengthwise*
- *1/2 cup - Corn kernels steamed*
- *1 and 1/2 to 2 cups - Mozzarella (pizza cheese) cheese grated*
- *2 cups - Pizza sauce*
- *4 – Pizza shells.*

Note:

- You may choose the vegetables and meats of your choice or can just have with cheese. Follow the same process.

Preparation and Cooking:

Now assemble pizzas.

- **Apply** pizza sauce generously on pizza shells. **Sprinkle** a little cheese over sauce. **Arrange** sliced vegetables or meat, or both artistically and finally **top** with grated cheese covering nicely.
- **Preheat** the CONVECTION mode of your microwave to 200 degrees Celsius for 5 minutes and **bake** pizzas in hot oven one by one for 10 minutes each. **Place** pizza on **high rack.**
  You can bake in hot electric or in cooking range oven as well.
- Remove the baked pizza.

***Pizza** is one of the important Italian breads which has become popular all over the world and is a craze with today's youth and even the growing ups under teens. It is made of flour / wheat flour dough and after being rolled is topped with tomato pizza sauce, vegetables/meats and mozzarella cheese. Ultimately baked in hot oven and served with herbs like oregano and chili flakes (opt). Mustard sauce is a good accompaniment to it.*

These days Pizza shells of all sizes (from king size to mini cocktail pizzas) can be bought like any other bread but you have to use your creativity in topping your pizza imaginatively.

To be continued

Serving:

Cut it into wedges with a pizza cutter and serve hot with Tomato sauce, Mustard sauce, Oregano and C hili flakes etc

Tips

*Prepared pizza/stored pizza can be reheated very well in the microwave. Place 1 full pizza, at room temperature, on double kitchen paper towel and **REHEAT** for 1.30 minutes.*

Some Interesting Information:

tlis believed "The **name Pizza** originated from the area around **Naples** (a way in the South-West Italy). It is not certain, however, that the nearby village of Pizza, where the flour for the best pizza dough is grown and grounded, can claim to be its creator. A pizza may first have been made to use up left-over bread dough and tomato sauce, plus whatever sausage, ham or cheese happened to be available" says the **Cordon Bleu book of 'Cheese and Savou ries'.**

- **Cooking time: 6 to 7 minutes for each pizza.**

Jalapeno Pizza

Mini Pizzas

Tender Hearts

Tender Hearts

Ingredients :

- *1 and ½ cup - Flour*
- *½ cup - Sugar*
- *1 tsp - Baking powder*
- *½ tsp - Baking Soda*
- *¼ tsp - Salt*
- *1/2cup - Butter*
- *3 to 4 tbsp - Milk*
- *2 tbsp - Milk powder*
- *1 tsp - Vanilla essence*

Preparation and Cooking:

- **Sieve together** flour, powder milk, baking powder, baking soda and salt in a trove.
- **Powder** sugar and mix with sieved flour.
- **Add** butter; mix with your finger tips till it resembles bread crumbs. **Add** milk and vanilla essence and mix.
- **Sprinkle** flour on a working surface and **roll** out the dough to 1/8th-inch thickness. **Cut** with heart shape cookie cutter. Take out as many cookies as possible. **Reroll** the remaining dough and cut cookies from that too.
- **Preheat** the **CONVECTION** mode of your microwave to **180 degrees Celsius** for 10 minutes. Or preheat your electric oven for 15 minutes for the same temperature for baking.
- **Place** the heart shape cookies in ungreased tray a little away from each other and **bake** in hot oven for 10 minutes. **STAND** the cookies in the oven for 3 to 5 minutes and then remove. **Cool and store** in a clean-dry jar, so that they remain crisp and crunchy.

Note : These heart shaped cookies or very tempting and just melt in mouth.

Serving:

Serve the cookies with any beverage. Or carry them in your tiffin-box.

Cooking time: 10 minutes

Tossed Baby Potatoes

Tossed Baby Potatoes

Ingredients :

- *600gm-Boiled and peeled Baby potatoes*
- *2tbsp-Cooking / olive oil*
- *1cup-Tomato sauce*
- *1tsp-Chili garlic sauce*
- *Salt-n-Pepper to taste*
- *Chaat masala to taste*
- *1/4 cup - Coriander chopped*
- *A few Toothpicks to serve on or small fruit forks to serve along.*

Preparation and Cooking:

- Wash and cook potatoes in the steaming basket on HIGH for 8 minutes and **stand** for 10 minutes and then **peel.**
- **Prick** the potatoes with a fork. **Place** them in a micro-safe dish with a lid. **Mix** oil, tomato sauce, chili garlic, salt and pepper.
- **Cover** and **HEAT** for 3 minutes, so that aroma of the sauces mingles well. **Open** the dish. **Sprinkle** chaat masala and coriander very well.

Serving:

Take out the potatoes in a serving dish and serve on toothpicks.

Cooking time: 20 minutes

Multi-coloured Pasta in Cheese Sauce

Multi-coloured Pasta in Cheese Sauce

Ingredients :

- *2cups - Pasta boiled*
- *2cups - Cheese sauce*
- *1/4cup - Cheese grated*
- *1/4cup Milk - (if needed)*
- *1 cup - Carrots chopped*
- *1/2 tsp - Oregano (opt)*
- *Green peas shelled*
- *Green pepper chopped (opt)*

Preparation and Cooking:

- **Grease** a micro-safe dish and keep aside.
- **Boil** carrots and peas in a steaming basket for 3 minutes on HIGH.
- **Combine** cheese sauce and oregano and mix with boiled pasta and vegetables. If you find the mixture, too thick, add milk and check the seasonings (salt-n-pepper).
- **Spread** the pasta mixture in the greased dish. Sprinkle grated cheese over it.
- Bake on **COMBINATION** mode. Press Combi-1, set time and start. Bake the dish for 15 minutes.
  Or bake in hot oven on **CONVECTION** mode for 30 minutes to get golden crust on top.

Serving:

Serve pasta in Cheese sauce as a meal.

__Classic pasta__ is made only with wheat, semolina and water. To __make Italian__ pasta dried wheat flour preparation. Mostly made from __durum wheat__ is used. The flour is well kneaded into stiff dough and forced through specially perforated cylinders from which it comes out in various shapes known by different names such as __macaroni, spaghetti,ditalini, crescioni, tagliatelli, tortellini, vermicelli, fusilli and far falla__ etc. Egg pasta is made by adding dry or fresh eggs to the same dough mixture. Some of them are tinged with vegetable colours too.

To be continued

Tips:

- *For this preparation pasta can be boiled beforehand, vegetables can also be steamed in advance and, of course, cheese sauce, too, can be cooked earlier. Mixing and baking can be done 30 minutes before the meal.*

- **White Sauce can be cooked on gas fire also nicely but it has to be cooked on slow fire for 20 min, stirring constantly, otherwise, raw smell of flour will be prominent.**

Health benefits:

Pasta is essentially an energy food providing the body with 350 calories per 100 gm pasta. It is also a cereal and contains carbohydrates and mineral salts, but very small amount of protein, fat and vitamins. Therefore, to make pasta a well balanced diet food value is added by using milk, variety of cheese, butter/olive oil, vegetables and meats etc which are seasoned with fresh and dry herbs, and all these ingredients provide enough protein, fats, vitamins and the dietary fibres to the meal.

Cooking time: 18 minutes micro cooking.

How to make
White sauce / Cheese sauce

Ingredients:

- 2 tbsp - Flour
- 2 tbsp - Butter
- 3cups - Milk
- 1/4 tsp leveled - Mustard powder
- Salt-n-pepper to taste.

Preparation and Cooking:

- Place butter in a micro-safe dish and heat it for 1 minute on HIGH, add sieved flour and stir. Cook on MEDIUM ie 80% heat for 2 minutes.
- Add lukewarm milk and whisk till the mixture turns smooth.
- Cook on MEDIUM for 7 minutes.
- Wear your gloves and remove the sauce from microwave. Add salt, pepper and mustard powder to the sauce. Add grated cheese. Mix. Cover and keep aside.

For Cheese sauce: Add 1/4 to1/2 cup grated cheese and mix thoroughly.
It will take about 25 minutes.

Mango Whip

Mango Whip

Ingredients :

- *3/4 tin - Condensed milk*
- *1/2 cup - Milk*
- *2 cups Cream*
- *1 cup - Mango cut into small pieces*
- *1 and 1/4 cup - mango pulp*
- *1/4 cup - chopped nuts*
- *1 tsp - Vanilla essence*
- *Cherries For garnishing.*

Preparation and Cooking:

- **Chill** cream under refrigeration.
- **Beat** condensed milk and milk together with an **electric hand beater.** Add mango pulp and mix.
- **Add** cream to condensed milk and **mango** mixture, and beat. Add essence and mix.
- **Freeze** mixture till half set. Remove from the freezer and **beat again. Add** mango pieces. **Freeze** till set properly. **Cut** into pieces and serve. **You may beat** with a fork till ice-cream is soft just before serving

Serving: Garnish with colourful sprinklers.

Variation: You may serve it with **Banana cream.** Make it while mango cream is setting and keep under refrigeration.

For Banana cream: Mix together 1 sliced - Banana, ½ cup - Fresh cream and ¼ cup - Powdered sugar and blend. Serve Mango Whip with **'banana cream'** and garnish with chopped nuts and Cherries.

Preparation time: 20 minutes and chilling time extra.

Pinwheel Sandwiches

Ingredients :

- *1 Loaf White or Brown Sandwich bread, cut lengthwise, not in traditional slices*
- *Any Sandwich spread of your choice such as Cheese spread, special sandwich spread or Jam/ Chocolate spread.*

Preparation and Cooking:

- **Cut** ends of bread and **lay it** flat Roll.
- **Spread** with sandwich spread generously and roll it up.
- **Wrap in cling wrap twice**; **place** in a zip-lock bag and **freeze** for 24 hours.
- **Remove** it from the freezer 1 hour before serving. **Cut** rolled sandwich in slices and refrigerate until used.

Note:

once the sandwiches are cut, always refrigerate until used. Sandwich will thaw within 1 hour.

Variation:

If the lengthwise cut bread is not easily available, so place 3 to 4 slices of trimmed bread in a vertical line overlapping So adjoining

Pinwheel Sandwiches

***A pinwheel** sandwich is a slice of bread that has been flattened with a rolling pin. The filling is added; the bread is rolled up; wrapped in cling wrap; cooled properly and then ultimately sliced to make small wheels.*

Pinwheel sandwiches are cute and the most fabulous finger food. Colourful cute little wheels are very versatile; great for tea-time; wonderful for kids' parties and elegant for the cocktails.

To be continued

ends; flatten with a rolling pin and crimp touching ends together. Spread filling and rollup bread carefully. Wrap and cool.

Serving:

Serve as and when required. Serve it as finger food for children anytime. You may serve pinwheel sandwiches as starters in children's party.

Tips:

Any well flavoured sandwich spread can be used for this dish. You may use Cheese, Chicken, Hard-boiled eggs, Turkey, Ham, finely grated vegetable paste mixed with butter/ cheese or mayonnaise.

Avoid using too moist spread. Any mixture should be of smoothly spreading consistency.

Preparation time: 25 to 30 minutes and chilling time extra.

Pinwheel Sandwiches

Swiss Roll / Jam Roll

Ingredients :

- *1 and 1/2 cup - Flour*
- *1 tsp - Baking powder*
- *1/4tsp - Salt*
- *3 Eggs*
- *1 cup - Sugar*
- *2 drops Vanilla essence*
- *1/3rd cup - Milk (warm)*
- *1/2 cup - Icing sugar*
- *1/2 cup - Mixed fruit Jam / Strawberry jam or 1 cup beaten cream mixed with sugar*
- *1/4 cup - Grated Chocolate*
- *1/2 cup - cream for serving (opt).*

Preparation and Cooking:

- **Prepare** a flat **baking tray**. **Line it** with paper and **grease** it well.
- **Powder sugar.**
- **Preheat** the oven to **180** degrees Celsius.
- **For making Sponge cake, sift** flour, salt and baking powder.
- **Beat eggs** with electric beater till **creamy** and slowly **mix in** powdered sugar and **beat** again.
- **Add** water and essence together and **beat;** mix in flour and beat. **Do not** over-mix.
- **Pour** it into a **greased** baking dish and **bake** for 20 minutes. **Remove** and **invert** over a kitchen towel **sprinkled** generously with **icing sugar.** Remove **the paper** when the cake is **still warm.** Roll the cake with **2" towel inside.** Cool the **sponge cake**

Chocolate Swiss Roll

Swiss roll is thin sponge cake, baked in a flat baking tray and then covered with Jam or chocolate sauce or even cream; and then rolled, chilled and sliced.

Jam Roll

To be continued

Step 1

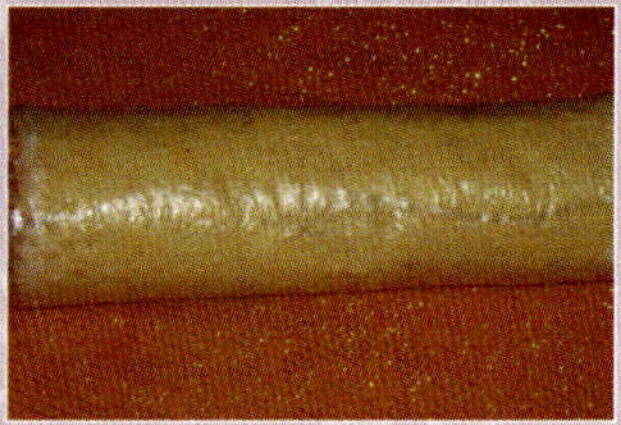

Step 2

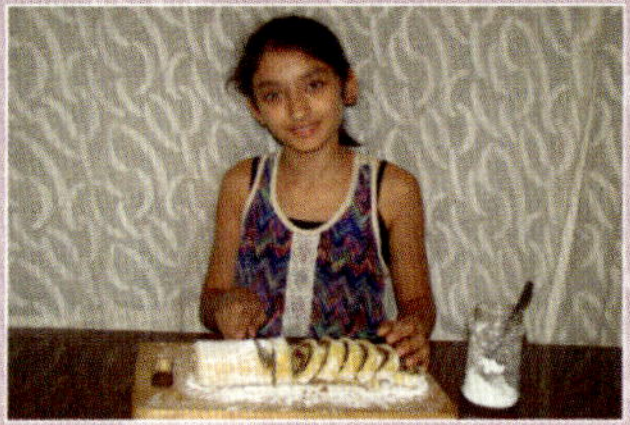

Step 3

Step 4

on the **cooling rack** outside the refrigerator.

- **Heat jam** with 1 to 2 tbsp water in it. **Mix** it well until **smooth. Unroll** the cake; **spread** jam carefully allover and **reroll it.** Or fill the cake with cream beaten over bowl of ice cubes till fluffy.
- **Wrap** it in cling **wrap** and **chill** it. **Slice** it into ½-inch thick slices before serving.

Serving:

Serve it any time with or without cream.

Tips:

Always measure sugar first (recommended in the recipe) and then powder.

Baking time: 20 minutes.

Yummy........

Yogurt Pancakes

Ingredients :

- *1 cup - Flour*
- *2 tbsp - Sugar*
- *1and ¼ tsp - Baking powder*
- *¼ tsp - Baking soda*
- *¼ tsp - Salt*
- *1 cup - Plain Yogurt*
- *2 Eggs*
- *2 tbsp - Melted butter / vegetable oil vor spray oil for cooking.*

Yogurt Pancakes

Preparation and Cooking:

- **Combine** all the dry ingredients in a bowl. **Make a well** in the centre and **break** the eggs in it and **whisk**; add yogurt and **stir** to mix properly. **Pour** in the melted butter or oil and **stir** once again. **Stand** the batter for 5 minutes.
- Meantime **heat a griddle** or large heavy bottomed frying pan.
- **Spray oil** on hot griddle and **spoon batter** into even cakes (you can place 3 to 4 pancakes with a distance in-between). And let them **cook for almost 2 minutes** on medium high flame or until bubbles form on the surface of cakes; **flip and cook** the other side too until **golden** brown.

*It is said, **'Eat your breakfast like a king, lunch like a common man and dinner like a pauper'.** Breakfast being the most important meal of the day, a dish like pancakes is just ideal to begin the day well with healthy spread. Pancakes are prepared in various ways, with milk, yogurt or buttermilk, and here we have selected yogurt to prepare it.*

Note:

This recipe will give you 8 to 10 pancakes.

To be continued

Serving:

Serve the pancakes hot either with Honey, Maple syrup, Molasses, Jam or with Strawberry / Blueberry sauce/ crush.

Variation:

Buttermilk pancakes or Milk pancakes are same as Yogurt pancakes, just use milk or butter milk instead of yogurt.
In the absence of buttermilk, you may combine part milk and part yogurt.
Instead of full quantity all purpose flour, you may use ¾ cup wheat flour and ¼ cup cornmeal or any other flour for texture and flavour.

Cooking time: Almost 5 minutes to cook each lot of 3 to 4 pancakes.

Yogurt Pancakes

Caramel Bananas with Vanilla Ice-cream

Caramel Bananas with Vanilla Ice-cream

Ingredients :

- *4 - Medium sized bananas*
- *1 tbsp - Butter*
- *½ cup - Sugar*
- *½ cup - Water*
- *1 tbsp - Brandy (opt)*
- *A few roasted Almonds or Pistachio nuts (opt)*
- *1 small pack Vanilla ice cream.*

Preparation and Cooking:

- **Heat** butter and sugar together in a pan on high fire till the sugar is fully cooked and is changing the colour to **brown**.
- **Lower** the heat and **add** water. **Simmer** for a few seconds.
- Meantime **peel and cut** bananas into halves lengthwise and **place** them in caramelized sugar syrup.
- **Add brandy**, if using, to the banana mixture. **Remove** from the fire and **cool** slightly.
- **Chop** the nuts.

Serving:

Place 1 halved banana in the serving plate; add 1 scoop or 1 square piece of ice-cream to the plate and drizzle some sauce over it. Garnish with the chopped nuts. Serve it immediately.

__Caramel__ is a liquid made by cooking sugar until it changes the colour it is used for flavouring and colouring food. For making caramel sauce a little water is added to caramelized sugar and cooked for a while. Any dessert flavoured with this sauce has unique taste.

To be continued

Tips:

to avoid de-colouration of the bananas, do not cut bananas in advance.

Health benefits of bananas:

Banana is considered nature's great snack . It is a fiber food and is good for heart, easy to digest and is powerhouse of nutrients. It is loaded with fiber both soluble and insoluble. It is a source of Potassium and Vitamin B6-that is easily digestible by the body. It s good for Blood pressure and helps fight Anemia.

Cooking time: 15 minutes.

Red Bananas

Raspberry Princess

Ingredients :

- *400 gm - Strawberry or Raspberry jelly crystals*
- *220 ml / 1 cup - Water*
- *2 cups - Vanilla ice-cream*
- *4 - Strawberries/raspberries for garnishing*
- *A few fresh mint or basil leaves for garnishing*
- *4 - Small glass bowls or glasses.*

Preparation and Cooking:

- **Put** the jelly crystals in a **micro-safe glass** bowl of medium size. **Add** water and **stir** properly.
- Cook in a microwave for 5 minutes, **uncovered**. Stir once after 3 minutes. **Take out** the bowl and **stir** once again gently as the syrup is hot.
- **Leave it to cool**. Refrigeration for 30 minute.
- Once the jelly mixture is cool, **beat it** with an electric hand beater. **Add vanilla ice cream** and beat till smooth in texture.
- **Spoon** it into glass bowls and **cover** with cling wraps or foil and **place** in the deep freezer for 1 hour.

Serving:

Garnish it with 1 spoon fresh cream, mint/basil leaves and fresh Raspberries. Serve it immediately as a dessert.

Raspberry Princess

*This simple mouth watering dish of **Raspberry jelly** crystals and **Vanilla ice cream**, not only is prepared fast, but consumed also very fast because of its sweet and sour deliciousness. This seasonal fruit is also known as **'golden berry'.***

To be continued

Note:
You may prepare it even with any other dark coloured jelly and name accordingly.

Health Benefits:
Like all the other berries, raspberries, too, contain valuable nutritional foods with great cleansing properties. They contain percentage of water ranging from 80 to 90 percent.

Raspberries are rich in potassium and other mineral elements; and contain valuable natural sugars which help cleansing the system.

Preparation and cooking : 30 minutes and chilling time extra.

Golden berry / Raspberry Fruit

Popeye's Favourite Ramekins
(Spinach and Corn Bake)

Popeye's favourite Ramekins

Ingredients :

- *1 bunch - Fresh Spinach*
- *1 tin - Cream style corn*
- *1 tsp leveled - Garlic paste*
- *1 tsp leveled - Ginger paste*
- *1tsp - Green chili paste or*
- *1/2 tsp - Black pepper powder*
- *1 tbsp - Fried onion-tomato paste*
- *2 cups - White sauce*
- *¼ cup - Grated cheese*
- *¼ cup - breadcrumbs*
- *Salt and pepper to taste.*

Preparation and Cooking:

- **Wash spinach** 3 times properly. **Microwave** spinach for 3 minutes for quicker cooking and retaining the lovely colour and most of the nutrients.
- **Preheat the oven** to 180 degrees Celsius.
- Remove spinach from microwave and **cool** slightly. **Grind** it in electric mixer and **keep aside**.
- **Mix together** white sauce and spinach. **Add** ginger- garlic paste, onion-tomato paste, green chili paste or pepper and salt; and **mix** well.
- **Take out** the cream style corn in a bowl and **mix** it well with a fork and **add** to spinach. Mix once again.

*Leafy green vegetable like **Spinach** with its delicate texture and jade green colour, provide more nutrients than any other food. Research shows that there are at least 13 flavonoid compounds in spinach that function as antioxidants and as anti-cancer agents. As such spinach is rich in Vitamin K, calcium and magnesium which boast bone health.*

To be continued

- **Grease a** baking dish with a **brush and pour** the spinach-corn mixture in it. Or **divide** the mixture into 4-5 ramekins as individual portions.
- **Mix together breadcrumbs** and grated cheese and **top** the dish with it.
- **Bake it** in the preheated oven for 25 to 30 minutes or until the cheese **is golden** and **bubbling**.

Serving: Serve it hot with toasts.

Cooking time: 45 minutes.

Fresh Corn on cob

Ginger Bread Man Cookies

Ginger Bread Man Cookies

Ingredients :

- *1 and ½ cup - Flour*
- *70gm - Butter*
- *1/4 cup - Brown sugar*
- *1/3 cup - Golden syrup*
- *1 - Egg yolk*
- *1 and ½ tsp - Ginger powder*
- *1/2 tsp - Cinnamon powder / all spice powder*
- *1 tsp - leveled Baking powder*
- *2 sheets of butter paper or thick plastic and a set of Ginger bread man / people shaped cookie cutter*
- *Baking tray lined with butter paper or a piece of aluminum foil*

For decoration:

- *1 - Egg white*
- *100gm - Icing sugar*
- *Colourful gems*
- *Sprinklers of your choice*
- *Edible colours/ tubes of edible writing gel*

Or instead of egg white use combination of 100gm - Butter 100gm - Icing Sugar.
Or use ½ cup - Fresh cream and 100 gm Icing sugar.

One of the popular cookies enjoyed by children like you.

Preparation and Cooking:

- **Preheat** the oven to 160 to 180 degrees Celsius.
- **Cream butter and brown sugar** together using electric beater.
- **Add egg yolk** and golden **syrup** and **mix** until combined.

To be continued

- **Sieve** flour and baking powder together and mix with the butter and sugar mixture. If it looks too dry add a spoon of **golden syrup** and knead the dough. It will be a little crumbly but it works.
- **Divide** the dough into 2 parts. **Roll** one part between the sheets of **butter paper** or plastic and **cut** out the desired shapes. Roll the second part the same way and cut the shapes. **Reroll** the cuttings of dough and use that too. **Place the** shaped cookies in the **baking tray** and **bake** for 10 minutes.
- **Switch off the oven** and with the help of an adult **take out** the cookie's tray and let them **cool**.
- Meantime **beat egg white** very stiff and **mix** icing sugar and 3 drops of **lemon juice**. **Divide** it into 2 to 3 **separate bowls** and mix 2 drops of desired colour. **Mix** well and **decorate** the cookies with **butter knives**.

Note:

You may apply white icing to the cookies and decorate with writing gels and other decorative smarties.

Baking time: 10 minutes.

Ginger Bread Man Cookies after decoration

Cheesy Omelet with Hard boiled Eggs

Ingredients :

- *4 - Eggs*
- *2 - Eggs boiled*
- *1/2 cup - Milk*
- *25gm - Cheese grated*
- *1/4 cup - Coriander chopped*
- *1 - Jalapeno green chili (opt)*
- *Salt-n-pepper to taste*
- *2 and 1/2 tbsp - Olive oil to cook the eggs*
- *1 small - Non-stick Egg pan to make omelets*

Cheesy Omelet with Hard boiled Eggs

Preparation and Cooking:

- **Split** and **deseed** the chili. **Cut** into small pieces. You may take help from an adult to chop chili. **Slice** boiled eggs in thick slices.
- **Beat each egg** separately with 1 tbsp milk, salt and pepper to taste. **Add** one spoon chopped coriander, 1 tbsp grated cheese and a few pieces of chopped chili. **Stir** well.
- **Heat 1** tsp oil in the egg pan on medium fire and **remove** it from fire. **Pour** beaten egg, saving a little, and **stir** with a **wooden spoon** evenly. **Place 2** slices of boiled egg and pour the saved beaten egg around. **Trickle** a few drops of oil over it and **cook** on medium fire till egg sets. **Turn the** omelet upside down and **switch off** the fire.
- After 1 minute **turn** the omelet into a plate. **Serve it** along with accompaniments of your choice.

Health benefits of Eggs:
Eggs are a very good source of high quality protein. They are not only tasty but also provide the energy to the body. The whites of eggs are rich source of selenium, vitamin D, B6, B12 minerals such as zinc, iron and copper. They contain all the daily vitamins and minerals needed to produce energy in all the cells of the body. Eating eggs is also good for bone, beauty and metabolism, brain and overall health.

To be continued

- The same way cook the remaining omelets for your siblings and friends.

Note:

Cheesy omelet is a good *item for the mini meals of growing up teen agers who are hungry all the time and need something nourishing and tasty.*

For variety you may add finely chopped and pre-boiled vegetables, such as carrot, beans and capsicum etc, and more cheese to your omelets.

If you are an egg lover, cook 2 eggs omelet for yourself.

Serving:

Serve the omelets with Bread and other accompaniments, such as Tossed vegetables, Potato wedges or French fries etc.

Cooking time: 6 to 10 minutes for each omelet.

Cheesy omelet in the pan

Rancheros

Rancheros

Ingredients :

- *8 - Soft corn tortillas*
- *8 - Eggs*
- *2 tbsp - Cooking oil*
- *1 and 1/4 cup - Delicious tomato sauce / Tomato salsa*
- *A piece of tomato and a little chopped or shredded cheese for decorating your Ranchero (opt)*

Preparation and Cooking:

- **Preheat a heavy based pan** over a medium heat; **brush** the tortillas with a little oil and **warm** in the pan from both sides. **Wrap** them in a kitchen napkin or a piece of foil to keep them warm.
- Now **brush** the pan generously with oil and **break 2 eggs** at a time in it and **cook over low heat till** the whites of the eggs are **set**.
- **Place 2** tortillas in a plate and **place** cooked eggs on top. **Spoon** tomato sauce **generously** covering the whites of the eggs and remaining part of **tortillas**.

Serving:

Decorate quickly if you like, otherwise serve it warm immediately.

*This classic **Mexican** breakfast dish is just ideal for those teenagers who love eggs in any form and in any meal. In this internationally famous dish, 2 single fried eggs are placed on a set of warmed Corn tortillas, then covered with delicious tomato sauce and served warm.*

To be continued

Tips:

Tortillas can be brought or prepared the previous day and stored under refrigeration. Even the sauce can be bought or cooked beforehand and stored. Warm it before use.

Note:

If the corn tortillas are not available in the market, they can be prepared at home with the domestic help. Mix together**1 and ½ cup maize flour** (makki-ka-atta) and **½ cup refined flour**; add a little **salt** and **knead** it with warm water to soft dough. **Divide** it in equal parts. Four fold a kitchen towel; **sprinkle** it with maize flour; **place** each ball over it and **roll into a thin disk**. **Brush** a griddle with a little oil and **cook tortillas** one by one from both sides. **Wrap** them in a napkin and **keep soft**. Store if needed be.

Cooking time: Almost 15 minutes to cook each set of tortillas.

Corn Tortillas

Bread Pudding Ramekins

Ingredients :

- *4 - White bread slices*
- *2 cups - Milk*
- *2 - Large eggs*
- *1/4cup - Sugar*
- *1tbsp - Melted butter*
- *1/2 tsp - Vanilla essence*
- *1/4cup - Sliced and roasted Almonds and Raisins (opt)*

Preparation and Cooking:

- **Cut the sides** of the bread slices and **break** into pieces. **Soak** it in the warm milk. Brush the ramekins cups lightly with melted butter
- **Brush** the ramekins cups lightly with melted butter
- **Break** eggs and beat nicely.
- **Preheat the oven** to 190 degrees Celsius.
- Now **mix together** milk with bread, beaten egg, melted butter and sugar and beat the mixture with an electric beater; **add** vanilla essence and mix again.
- **Fill** the ramekins 3/4th with the mixture; **sprinkle** some nuts over and **place** the bowls in the **baking tray**; and **bake** till the pudding is **set** and **golden** in colour.
- **Remove** the tray from the oven wearing the gloves.

Serving: Serve the pudding warm.

Cooking time: 12 to 15 minutes.

Bread Pudding Ramekins

Quick dessert made of eggs, milk, bread and sugar is not only tasty but very healthy, too, for the growing children. It is so easy that children can handle it easily and enjoy it too. It is an ideal dessert for the cold weather.

Ramekin is a small dish in which food can be baked (without a lid) and served too.

Fruit Kebabs

Fruit Kebabs

Ingredients :

- *12 - Strawberries*
- *3 - Cheese cubes*
- *12 - Black grapes*
- *6 - Bamboo skewers to serve fruit on*
  Or Take different fruits such as Grapes, pieces of Mango, Pineapple and Paneer cubes (instead of Cheese)etc.
- ***Dip: 2** tbsp Honey*
- *2 tbsp Lemon juice*
- *1/4 tsp Lemonrind (opt)*
- *Salt and Pepper to taste.*

Preparation and Cooking:

- **Mix all the ingredients** mentioned for dip together thoroughly in a small bowl and **refrigerate** covered.
- **Cut** cheese cubes into 4 pieces each and strawberries into halves; and **thread** on skewers alternately.
- **Arrange the skewers** in the serving plate, cover with cling wrap or foil loosely and cool for 30 minutes before serving.

Serving: Serve the Fruity Kebabs along with its dip. You may give the individual plates to your friends / family to enjoy the fruity kebabs along with dip.

Tips : For more quantity double the recipe.

Preparation time: 30 to 40 minutes.

They say, 'it's good to eat five different kinds of fruits and vegetables every day to maintain the good body and mind and your body needs lots of these to keep you healthy'.

Fresh fruit / cubes served along with Cheese / Paneer pieces on skewers make excellent starters. Even Cucumbers cut into cubes and served along with Pineapple pieces and Cherry tomatoes are interesting and easy. The sweet-tangy dip made of honey and lemon enhances the taste and curtails the sweetness of the fruits.

Chicken Sweet-corn Soup

Ingredients :

- *1tin – Cream style sweet-corn, 4 cups – Water*
- *1/4 cup – Corn flour/corn startch*
- *1 – Large egg (opt)*
- *2 tsp leveled - Salt*
- *1/2 tsp – White pepper powder*
- *1/4 cup – Fresh sweet-corn kernels*
- *1- Soup cube*
- *1 cup boiled and chopped boneless chicken*

Chicken Sweet-corn Soup

Accompaniments:

Soy sauce, Vinegar,
Chili sauce (opt) for
flavouring the soup and
1 cup – crisp fried noodles to
serve along (opt)

*One of the most popular **Chinese soups** enjoyed by the majority of children in India, as it is bland and it can be spiced easily according to your taste.*

Preparation and Cooking:

- **Open the cream style corn tin** and take out the contents in a bowl. With a fork **break the soft lumps** of cream style corn. **Place** it in a deep pan and **add 4** cups water. **Mix** it nicely. **Break** the soup cube and **add** to the pan
- **Break egg** and beat it. **Keep** it aside.
- **Mix** corn-flour with ½ cup water and **keep aside.**

To be continued

- Now **place** the pan on fire and **boil** the contents. **Add** fresh corn kernels, salt and pepper. **Simmer** the soup for 5 minutes if preparing vegetarian soup.

Note: *At this point add chicken to the soup if making chicken corn soup.*

Serving: With the help of a ladle divide the soup into 4 bowls and serve it hot. Place the accompaniments on the table and add to your bowl according to your taste and enjoy it.

Sweet corn and vegetables soup

Tips:

*If you prefer **Vegetable corn soup,** add 1 cup boiled chicken to the boiling soup at step 4. Use chicken soup cube instead of veg soup cube as taste maker and omit Chicken .*

Cooking time: 20 to 25 minutes.

Accompaniments to the soups

Crispy Crunchy Noodles Salad

Ingredients :

- *2 cups - Crisp fried noodles*
- *1 small - Green pepper*
- *1 small - Red pepper*
- *2 - Spring onions*
- *1 - Jalapeno (opt)*
- *1 small - Cucumber*
- *1 medium - Carrot*
- *1medium - Tomato*
- *2 leaves Purple cabbage.*

Seasonings:

Vinegar
Lemon
Soy sauce
Chili sauce
Salt and Pepper

Preparation and Cooking:

- **Wash, clean and chop** vegetables into small pieces.
- **Mix together** all the seasonings in a small bowl and **keep aside.**
- In a serving bowl **combine together** crisp noodles and vegetables and **toss** properly.
- In a serving bowl **place** crisp noodles and **pour** over the mixed vegetables and seasonings. Gently **stir** with a fork and **serve** immediately.

Serving: Serve to satiate/ satisfy the small evening hunger. Its healthy and tasty.

Preparation time: 30 minutes.

Crispy Crunchy Noodles Salad

Tip: *Keep the noodles, veggies and seasonings ready but combine and mix a few minutes before serving, so that crunchiness in the salad is retained.*

Peas-Potato Rolls

Ingredients :

- *500gm - Potatoes boiled*
- *1 cup – Green peas shelled and boiled.*

Seasonings:

1 and 1/2 tsp - Salt	*1/4 cup - Bread crumbs*
1/2 tsp – Pepper powder	*1 - Egg*
1/4 tsp - Ginger powder	*1 cup - Crushed corn flakes*
1/2 tsp - Mango powder	*Oil for frying*
1/2 tsp - Garam masala	

Preparation and Cooking:

- **Grate potatoes** in a trove (paraat).
- **Crush green peas** lightly and **add** to the grated potatoes.
- Now **add** all the dry **ingredients**, except corn flakes.
- **Break** and beat egg and mix with the potato mixture. Now **mix** the potato mixture with hand and **make smooth dough**.
- **Divide** the dough into 12 portions and **shape** into rolls.
- **Spread** the crushed cornflakes into a plate and **roll** each portion in it.
- **Get help from the elder** person and heat oil in a frying pan to the

Peas-Potato Rolls

*For hundreds of years nutritious **green-peas** are relished in numerous ways. Mostly mixed with other vegetables and rice prepations, peas are popularly eaten all over the world. Peas contain Fiber and Antioxidants. They have high protein contents. They also contain vitamin A, K and C.*

Green-peas actually belong to the Family of Legumes such as Lentils, Chick peas and beans etc.

To be continued

smoking point.

- Now **lower** the heat and **fry 2** to 3 portions at a time till rolls are golden brown. Take them out with a slotted spoon and **place** in a plate lined with kitchen paper.

Serving: Serve them hot with Tomato sauce or Fresh green chutney.

Cooking time: 40 minutes.

Fresh green Peas

Indian Roti / Phulka and Parathas
(Basket of Indian Breads)

Ingredients :

Basic Atta / dough:

- *1 cup - Wheat flour*
- *1/4 cup - water / milk*
- *1-pinch - salt*
- *1 tsp - cooking oil*

Preparation and Cooking:

- In a trove **combine** wheat flour, salt and cooking oil **make** a well in the **center** and **add water** or milk and mix with your fingers. Now **knead it** with the hands till the dough is smooth. Cover it with a damp kitchen napkin and let it stand for 30 minutes.
- **Divide it** into lemon sized balls.
- **Heat tava**/ griddle on high flame and lower the heat.
- **Roll each ball** properly; **dip in** dry flour; **flatten** with your fingers and finally **roll it** with the rolling pin into a disk.
- **Pick it** up; **dust** away the extra dry flour and **put gently** on the preheated griddle. **Change the side** when the disk changes a little colour. **Increase** the flame and **cook** chapatti from the other side too, till it **develops the freckles**. Now **press the sides** of chapatti with a **folded duster** and it will puff.
- **Remove it** and store in a casserole lined with a clean duster.
- Thus **finish rolling** and **cooking** all the chapattis.

Indian Roti

***Wheat** is one of the most common cereals that human eat since time immemorial. It is a vehicle for vitamins and minerals. It is a source of Carbohydrates, Fiber, Magnesium, B vitamins, Folic acid and Antioxidants. These nutrients contribute positively to our health. Eating wheat provides energy to the body that is essential for us to go through our daily routine.*

It is the staple food in large part of Northern Zone of India**. A large variety northern dishes, sweets and savouries are prepared with wheat flour and other wheat products such as semolina and refined flour. **Chapatis, Parathas** and **Puries** are most popular items and they are cooked almost daily three times a day in Indian households for breakfast, lunch and dinner. **Here we are introducing you to basic breads (phulka/paratha) cooked in day to day life.

To be continued

- ***Note:*** For plain paratha after step no. 1, apply ghee/cooking oil on the disk. Fold it half, apply a little ghee and fold into half again; dip into dry atta and roll. Cook on medium fire on hot tava; applying ghee on both sides till and cook till crisp from both sides and then serve.

Variations:

A. Meethi Choi:

Ingredients : *Basic atta – Equal to 1 tennis ball (for 1 roti), 1tbsp- Ghee / cooking oil, 2 tbsp– Sugar and ¼ tsp fennel seeds (saunf).*

Meethi Roti

Cooking:

- **Heat** clean tava / griddle and **lower** the heat.
- **Roll** the basic wheat dough and **apply** 1 tsp ghee/oil; **place** sugar in the centre; **sprinkle** fennel seeds and **fold** all the sides of rolled chapatti in the centre. **Sprinkle dry flour** on the working surface and **roll** with the rolling pin evenly, so that **sugar spreads** nicely.
- **Place** the rolled roti gently on tava. Increase the heat. Cook till the chapatti turns its colour lightly, and now again reduce the heat. Spread 1 tsp fat evenly over it and turn the meethi roti once with the help of a flat spoon. Spread the last teaspoon of ghee and turn it. After a while remove the crisp caramelized roti. Cool a bit and cut into four parts.

Serving: Serve it as a dessert or eat it any time to enjoy the sweet thing.

To be continued

B. Green Spinach Paratha:

Ingredients : *1 cup – Wheat flour + ¼ cup – Gram flour, ½ cup - Spinach puree, 1 tsp – Salt, 1/8 to ¼ tsp - Red chili powder, 1 pinch of Ajwain, 1 pinch ginger powder and 1 tbsp- Cooking oil or ghee.*

Spinach Parathas

Preparation and Cooking:

- **Combine** all the ingredients for **Green paratha** in a trove and mix to convert into **soft dough.** If dough is hard, **sprinkle** a few drops of milk/water to make it pliable.
- Roll and cook it like plain paratha from both sides and enjoy **the goodness of spinach as well as whole wheat flour with curds or white butter.**

C. Red Tomato-Chili Paratha:

Ingredients : *1 cup – Wheat flour, ¼ cup – Onion-Tomato paste, 2 tbsp – Tomato puree, 1 tsp – Salt, ¼ tsp - Red chili powder, 1 pinch of Ajwain, 1 pinch - Ginger powder and 1 tbsp - Cooking oil.*

Tomato paratha

Preparation and Cooking:

- **Combine** all the ingredients for **Red paratha** in a trove and **mix** to convert into soft dough. If dough is hard, **sprinkle** a few drops of milk/water to make it pliable.
- **Roll and cook** it like plain paratha from both sides, **applying ghee/oil** till crisp and well done. You can't resist the temptation of having it.

Cooking time: Each paratha takes about 3 to 4 minutes.

Jelly Cups

Ingredients :

Choose any jelly - from different flavours such as Strawberry
Raspberry
Apple
Mixed fruit
Black currant
Pineapple and Mango jelly etc.

- *100 gm- Any jelly crystals*
- *500 ml - Water*

Preparation and Cooking:

- **Boil** water in a pan; **remove** from fire and **add** jelly crystals. **Stir** properly and **place** on fire to cook till the **crystals** are **dissolved** and jelly is **clear. Cool.**
- **Place under refrigeration** for 30 minutes and **pour** in the serving cups/ glasses you like and **place** in the **coldest** place of a refrigerator for **1 hour** or till sets properly.

Serving: Eat it as such or with a little cream (if you like) or ice cream.

Variation : Cook jelly crystals with 250 ml water; cool and set under refrigeration, for example, Black currant jelly.

When jelly is half set, place it in a liquidizer; mix 200 ml fresh plain yogurt or fresh cream; churn for a while and set in separate small bowls or glasses for 1 hour under refrigeration.

Cooking time: 15 minutes for cooking and chilling time extra.

Pineapple Jelly With Cream & Fruit

Apple Jelly

Mango Jelly

Black Currant jelly mixed with cream

Hotdogs and Burgers

Ingredients :

- *6 - Hotdog Buns*
- *6 to 8 - Vegetable rolls / ready to eat*
- *Chicken sausages*
- *1/2 cup - Tomato salsa or sauce*
- *1/4 cup – Cheese grated*
- *1/4 cup - Coriander chopped (opt)*

Preparation and Cooking:

- **Slit a hotdog bun** length wise from the centre without separating the bottom.
- **Heat** vegetable rolls or ready to eat sausages in a microwave for 30 seconds, covering them with paper towels.
- **Apply sauce**/salsa with a butter knife or a palate knife.
- **Place** one roll or a chicken sausage in the **centre**. If the bun is longer you can cut a piece of roll or sausage and place along.
- Sprinkle a few leaves of coriander if you like. **Sprinkle grated cheese** or add cheese spread from a tube.

Serving:

Serve it as a snack or whenever needed to satisfy a little hunger.

Hotdogs and Burgers

Hotdogs and Burgers *are the most popular snacks/ mini meals consumed by the present generation all over the world. They just grab it quickly and walk away. But the same items can be taken at home in a relaxed manner along with a good cup of soup or a serving of a salad. Though these items are considered as junk food but balancing them with healthy food items can be a good treat to yourselves and your peer group.*

To be continued

Variation:

You may serve hotdogs with fresh salad tossed with a little mayonnaise sauce and or with baked-beans as a complete meal.

Burger with Soybeans Patties

For Burgers you need: *6 – Potatoes or mix veg/non-veg burger pattice, 6 - Burger buns, 6- Salad leaves, 6 – Thinly sliced Tomato pieces, 6 – thinly sliced Onion pieces, 6 – Cheese slices (opt), Tomato sauce or Green chutney (opt), 6 leaves. – Lettuce washed and dried on kitchen towel*

Cut burger buns into 2 parts; on one part of the bun **place** one leaf of lettuce, slice of tomato, one burger pattice, one slice onion and slice of cheese. Cover it with the other half of the bun; **press it down** and **insert** a toothpick in the centre, so that it can be held properly. If you like **wrap** it in tissue paper and just **place** in a micro oven for **30 seconds**. Cheese will melt slightly and burger will also be warmed.

Serving: Serve immediately with sauce / chutney in individual plate. You may serve it as part of the mini meal. Tossed salad, any hot Soup and some Potato chips are the best accompaniments.

Note: Burger pattice can be made of potatoes, mix vegetables, meats, fish fillets or of Soya granules.

Assembling time: 30 minutes.

Pastry Platter
(pineapple, strawberry,chocolate)

Pineapple Pastry
Ingredients :

- *1 - Sponge cake*
- *250 gm - Fresh cream*
- *2 drops - Pineapple essence*
- *5 to 6 slices - Tinned Pineapple*
- *1/2 cup - Liquid*
- *2 tbsp - Icing sugar.*

Preparation and Cooking:

- **Chill the cream** in the deep freezer and **beat** it till thick and starts forming shape. Immediately **add** icing sugar and pineapple essence. **Keep it in on pan of ice** or under refrigeration.
- **Chop pineapple** into small pieces.
- **Level cake** top and **cut** it into 2 parts from the centre lengthwise.
- **Spread** one of the parts on a flat plate or tray and **sprinkle** pineapple juice generously from the tin. **Repeat** the process with the second part too.
- **Take out the cream** and spread it on cakes with a palate knife. **Spread** a layer of chopped pineapple on one of the cake parts.
- Now **gently lift** the second part and place the cream side down on **top of** the pineapple layer.

Pineapple Pastry

Note: *The recipe of the Sponge cake has been written in the dish called* ***Swiss roll/Jam roll.*** *Bake cake in a rectangular or square cake tin.*

To be continued

- **Sprinkle** some pineapple juice on top also.
- **Spread cream** generously on top and **smoothen** it with palate knife. **Place** chopped pineapple evenly on top and **garnish** the way you like, or with cherries / pistachio nuts for contrast for example.
- **Keep under refrigeration** for chilling, and that will allow the cream to set nicely.
- **Cut** into desired size pieces **and serve** as a snack or a dessert.

Chocolate Pastry

Ingredients :

- *1 - Sponge cake*
- *250 gm – Fresh cream*
- *3/4 cup – Chocolate sauce*
- *2 drops – Chocolate essence*
- *3/4 cup – Grated chocolate or chocolate chips*
- *2 tbsp – Icing sugar (opt).*

Chocolate Pastry

Preparation and Cooking:

- **Chill** the cream in the deep freezer and **beat** it till thick and starts forming shape. Immediately **add** icing sugar and chocolate essence. **Keep** it in on pan of ice or under refrigeration.
- **Warm chocolate sauce** with 2 tbsp water.
- **Level** cake top and cut it into 2 parts from the centre length-wise.
- **Spread** one of the parts on a **flat plate** or tray and **sprinkle** chocolate sauce. **Repeat** the process with other half of the cake too.

To be continued

- **Take out the cream** and spread it on cakes with a **palate knife**. Now gently **lift** the second part and **place** the cream side down **on top**.
- **Sprinkle chocolate sauce** on top also. Now **cover** the top with generous layer of beaten cream.
- Decorate the top with chocolate chips or grated chocolate or chocolate curls (if available).
- **Keep** under refrigeration for **chilling**, and that will allow the cream to set nicely.
- **Cut** into desired size pieces **and serve** as a snack or a dessert

Strawberry or Blueberry Pastry

Ingredients :

- *1 - Sponge cake*
- *250 gm – Fresh cream*
- *1/2 cup - Strawberry / Blueberry crush*
- *A few fresh – Strawberries or blueberries (if possible).*

Strawberry Pastry

Preparation and Cooking:

- **Chill** the cream in the deep freezer and **beat it** till thick and starts forming shape. **Keep it** in on pan of ice or under refrigeration.
- **Level cake top** and cut it into 2 parts from the centre lengthwise.
- **Warm berry crush** with 4 tbsp water, stirring well.

To be continued

- **Spread** one of the parts on a **flat plate** or tray and **sprinkle berry sauce**. **Repeat** the process with other half of the cake too.
- **Take out** the cream and spread it on cakes with a palate knife. Now **gently lift** the second part and **place** the cream side down on top.
- Sprinkle berry sauce on top also. Now cover the top with generous layer of beaten cream.
- Slice strawberries and decorate the pastry with fresh strawberry pieces.
- **Keep under refrigeration for chilling**, and that will allow the cream to set nicely.
- **Cut** into desired size pieces **and serve** as a snack or a dessert

Serving: Cut the chilled pastry into desired size pieces and serve as a snack or a small portion of dessert.

Note: You may serve the pastry as a cake also

Fruit Cups
(Shortcrust Pastry)

Fruit Cups

Ingredients :

- *1 recipe - Tarts pastry*
- *1 cup – Plain custard*
- *1 cup chopped mixed fruits (such as apple, pear, grapes, strawberry, kiwi or blue berry etc)*

Preparation and Cooking:

- Make tarts according to the instructions of the recipe. Mix chopped fruits (saving some for garnishing) with custard and cool under refrigeration. Fill the tart shells with prepared custard with a spoon and garnish according to your imagination. Now enjoy the fruit tarts.

Serving: Serve the tart shells as a dessert or at your special gathering.

For making custard: Boil 300 ml milk with 1 tbsp sugar. Mix 1 tbsp leveled corn-flour with ¼ cup milk and pour into boiled milk; stir well; and cook on slow fire till it starts coating the spoon. Remove from fire and cool.

Variation: Fill the cups (tarts) with any savoury filling and serve as starters. Or you may bake one single big tart; cool and fill up with lukewarm filling. Cut the pastry into wedges and serve.

Note: *The recipe of tart pastry/ tart shells has been written in the dish named **'Apple tarts'**.*

Cooking time: Depends on your planning, if your custard is precooked, then within 35 to 40 minutes you can bake your tarts and finally assemble.

Kiwi Delight / Souffle

Kiwi Delight

Ingredients :

- *1 and ½ cup – Milk*
- *3- Eggs*
- *3 tbsp – Sugar*
- *1 tbsp leveled - Corn flour*
- *3/4 cup – Water*
- *1/4 cup – Gelatin*
- *4 tsp – Gelatin*
- *1 or 2 kiwis for garnishing*
- *1 – Jelly mould*
- *2 trays of ice*
- *2 bottles of cold water and a shallow bowl /trove to hold ice and water*

Preparation and Cooking:

- **Prepare the jelly mould.** Brush the jelly mould with cooking oil from inside. Rinse under water without touching the inside. Shake well and place the bowl in the freezer.
- **Make egg custard** and cool. Separate egg yolks and whites.
- **Mix together** egg yolks, sugar, corn flour and milk together and beat. Cook over a pan of hot water (or use double boiler) on medium fire and keep stirring with a wooden spoon till custard starts thickening and coats the back of the spoon.
- **Boil** 1 cup water. **Mix gelatin** with 4 tbsp water in a small bowl and place in the bowl of hot water till the **crystals dissolve** and gelatin is transparent in appearance. Remove from water and pour gelatin in custard.

Health benefits:

Kiwi is loaded with nutrients such as Vitamin-C, Vitamin-K, Vitamin-E, Potassium and minerals. It also has antioxidants and dietary fibers. Even its black seeds are edible. Its other health benefits are the following:

It improves the digestive system; relives from insomnia and is good for diabetes; it is also beneficial during pregnancy and promotes the healthy skin.

To be continued

- **Put water and ice** in the trove and place the custard bowl in it to cool the custard. Mix kiwi crush and ¼ cup water. Once the custard is cold enough, pour the kiwi crush in it and keep stirring.
- **Beat the egg whites very stiff** and fold into the cold custard till it is properly mixed.
- **Remove** the jelly mould from the freezèr and pour the prepared custard in it and place the mould again in the deep freezer for1 hour or till set. Remove from freezer and keep it in the coldest part of a refrigerator till used. Place a serving plate in the refrigerator.
- **Un-mould / de-mould** the Kiwi soufflé onto the cold plate.
- **For un-moulding** , loosen the ends of the dish with a palate knife, then place a cold plate on the soufflé mould and invert. Tap the mould gently and pick up the mould. with lukewarm filling. Cut the pastry into wedges and serve.
- This delightful dessert is prepared on the fashion of soufflé. It is very light in texture and soothing in taste.

Serving : Garnish the soufflé with Kiwi slices and serve. You may cut it in wedges. If you like you can serve a little fresh cream over each portion.

Tips: *By chilling the mould before hand, you save on the chilling time of the dish. If the dish is to be served later or next day, do cover it with cling wrap and store in the colder part of your refrigerator. Not only the brilliant green colour of this exotic fruit- Kiwi is soothing to the eyes but its sweet tangy taste also provides the unique taste. Kiwi, originally, is native of Chiana. Later the first seeds were brought out of Chiana by the missionaries to New Zealand at the turn of this century.*

Preparation time: 30 minutes, chilling time extra.

Chicken ham and Cheese Sandwich

Ingredients :

- *8 slices - White bread*
- *2 slices - Cheese singles*
- *4 slices - Chicken ham*
- *1/4 cup – Mayonnaise*
- *1/4 cup – Tomato sauce*
- *¼ cup – Green chutney / pesto sauce*
- *1 tbsp - Mustard sauce (opt)*
- *4 - Salad leaves*

Preparation and Cooking:

- **Mix** mustard sauce with mayonnaise (if using mustard sauce)and apply on 4 slices; apply tomato sauce on 2 slices and green chutney on remaining 2 slices.
- Now **assemble** into 2 sets. Place 1 piece of chicken ham between 2 slices applied with mayonnaise and place salad leaf too; **apply sauce** on top of second slice also and place a cheese slice; then top it with third slice smeared with green chutney, **apply green chutney** on other side of slice too; cover it with 2nd leaf of lettuce and chicken ham slice and **finally top** with a slice having mayonnaise on.
- **Insert 1 tooth pick** temporarily in the centre of 4 pieces assembled into 1 set; **press lightly** with your palm and **cut the brown sides** of the sandwich. Cut the sandwich into desired shape. **Repeat the process** with the other set too.

Chicken ham and Cheese Sandwich

Chicken ham, *the flat slices of chicken meat is made from top quality breast meat. It is treated and smoked and that enriches its test.*

Not only ham slices are ideal for sandwiches, but ham is eaten in various ways such as salads and soups too.

To be continued

Serving: Serve it at meal time with any soup or salad as a meal. You may enjoy it when you are really hungry.

Tips: *If you are preplanning to make sandwiches for yourself or any friends or relatives, to be consumed later, in that case wrap the sandwiches in a moist napkin or in cling-wrap and store in a flat type box under refrigeration till used.*

Variations: You can also use softened butter instead of mayonnaise, cheese spreads, variety of jams, thick green chutney & chocolate paste etc to apply on bread slices. Instead of chicken ham, thin slices of vegetables such as cucumber and tomatoes can be used along with cheese.

Preparation time: 20 to 30 minutes.

Triangle sandwich

Round sandwich

Square sandwich

Cheese Toasts

Cheese Toasts

Ingredients :

- *16 slices - Sandwich bread*
- *2 cups - grated Cheese*
- *1/2 cup - Butter at room temperature*
- *2 tbsp - Milk*
- *4 green - Chilies (opt)*
- *1 tsp - Pepper powder*
- *Fresh Coriander chopped - 1/4 cup*

Preparation and Cooking:

- **Deseed** green chilies (if you are using) and **chop** them fine. **Combine** cheese, butter and pepper in a bowl and mix with a fork; add chopped chilies and coriander, too.
- Now **spread** the cheese mixture on all the slices.
- **Place** 3 to 4 slices at a time on grilling rack. **GRILL** each batch for 6 minutes. **Repeat** the process of grilling with remaining toasts.
- Take out the toasts; **cut** into rectangles or squares.

Serving: Serve them hot as a snack, for breakfast or as starter.

Cooking time: **6 to 7 minutes for grilling each lot.**

Always Pre-heat the grill or oven before Toasting, Roasting and Baking.

Coconut Macroons

Ingredients :

- *1 cup – Flour/maida*
- *3/4 cup – Desiccated coconut*
- *1/3 cup – Butter*
- *1 tsp – Vanilla essence*
- *1 – Egg*
- *1cup – Soft brown sugar*
- *1 tsp – Baking powder*
- *A pinch – salt*
- *A few glazed cherries (opt)*

Preparation and Cooking:

- **Melt butter** in a working bowl; add sugar immediately; beat with electric beater; add egg and beat well.
- **Add desiccated coconut** and vanilla. Mix.
- **Preheat your electric oven/** convection mode of your microwave oven or oven part of cooking range to 180 degrees Celsius.
- **Sieve together** flour, baking powder and salt; and add to the sugar coconut mixture. Mix together. If you find the mixture too thick, add a few drops of luke-warm milk.
- **Put 1 tbsp of batter** in each cavity of muffin tin or in tart cups; place half a cherry on each cavity and **bake for 15 to 17 minutes.** Remove from oven and cool. Take out macaroons with a butter knife or a palate knife gently.

Cooking time: 35 to 40 minutes

Coconut Macroons

A light biscuit made with egg, sugar, coconut and ground alomnds (opt) its called Macroon. It is also spelled as Macaron.

Ideally, Macarons can be served with any hot or cold beverage.

Fish Cakes

Fish Cakes

Ingredients :

- *500 gm - Boneless fish (such as Basa)*
- *1 - Lemon*
- *2 - Medium sized boiled potatoes*
- *Fresh bread crumbs - From slices of regular bread*
- *1 tsp - Chaat masala*
- *1/4 tsp – Black pepper powder*
- *1/4 tsp – Ginger powder*
- *1/4 tsp – Garam masala*
- *1/4 tsp – Chopped Coriander leaves*
- *1/4 tsp – Red chili powder (opt)*
- *1 tsp or to taste – Salt*
- *Oil for frying*
- *10 to 12 – Peppercorns*

Preparation and Cooking:

- **Squeeze lemon and apply juice to the fish**, and let it **stand for** 30 to 40 minutes to remove the **fishy smell.**
- **Strain the** liquid and **place** the fish in steaming basket with ¼ cup water underneath. Micro cook fish for 5 minutes. **Remove** from the oven and **cool** the fish.
- Meantime **grate** boiled potatoes and **place** in a trove. **Mix** all the dry ingredients. **Mash fish** and add to the **potato mixture**. Now **mash** everything together to soft dough, and **divide** into equal sized balls.

Fish a high protein and low fat food *is considered one of the best non-vegetarian items on this planet*

it is light on stomach and just get digested within 1 hour, where as chicken takes 2 hours to be digested and mutton (Lamb etc) takes 3 hours.

To be continued

Note: This recipe will give you approximately 10 to 12 fish cakes.

- Now **roll each ball** like a sausage and **shape** like fish. **Insert** 1 peppercorn at the place **of eye**. **Turn** all the balls into **fish shape.**
- **Line a** plate with a paper napkin.
- With the help of a grown up person **heat oil** in a frying pan / kadai to the smoking point; **reduce the heat** and fry one fish cake at a time on medium fire. Take it out of oil with a **perforated spoon** and place on a plate **lined** with paper napkin. **Fry** remaining fish cakes too in the similar fashion.

Fish Cakes-unfried

Serving: Enjoy it anyway as a snack or as a part of a mini meal with Chips / Salad or Soup and Bread etc.

Tips:

- *Marinating fish with lemon juice or vinegar removes the fishy smell.*
- *Placing fried items on paper towels immediately after taking out of hot oil, helps in absorbing the extra fat from fried food.*

Health benefits of eating fish: Fish is the one of the best source of nutrients that are incredibly important for the body and brain. Fish is the best source of Omega-3 fatty acids. Not only it is loaded with protein but also with Vitamin-D.it is also rich in calcium and phosphorus and a great source of minerals such as iron, zinc, iodine, magnesium and potassium. it boosts the heart condition and reduces the cholesterol. Some people believe that it boosts the mood too. It must be eaten two to three days a week, if not daily.

Cooking time: 1 hour.

Yummy Shakes and Smoothies

Kiwi Smoothie :

Ingredients :

- *3 - Kiwis*
- *1 - Banana of medium size*
- *1and ½ cup - Milk*
- *2 tbsp - Sugar*

Preparation and Cooking:

- **Put** peeled and chopped banana and kiwis into a blender
- **Add** sugar and milk; and **blend** until smooth.
- P**our** into glasses and **top** with a slice of kiwi.

Serving: Serve at once.

Variation: Instead of milk, add readymade lemonade and then blend. After pouring into glasses serve it with 1 to 2 tbsp strawberry ice cream.

Strawberry Bliss:

Ingredients :

1 cup - fresh / frozen strawberries

1 and 1/4 cup - Full cream (whole) milk

1 to 2 tbsp - Sugar

Sliced strawberries and fresh mint leaves for garnishing-optional.

Kiwi and banana smoothy

Smoothies** belong to the family of milkshakes which are wonderfully **refreshing and nourishing.** They give instant **energy** too. They are free **from preservatives** and artificial coloring; quick to make; look fabulous; cool in nature and just ideal for growing up kids, because milkshakes are a good source of **Calcium.

To be continued

Preparation and Cooking:

- **Put** all the ingredients except chopped strawberry and mint in a blender and **process** until smooth.
- **Pour** the strawberry shake into glasses and decorate

Serving: Serve immediately.

Tips: *In summer months, a few ice cubes can be added additionally while blending if the strawberries are fresh.*

Strawberry Bliss

Delicious Chocolate Milkshake:

Ingredients :

- *1cup – Milk,*
- *2 tbsp – Chocolate syrup,*
- *1/3 cup – Chocolate ice cream,*
- *Grated chocolate to decorate - Optional*

Preparation and Cooking:

- Pour the milk and chocolate syrup into a blender and blend.
- Add the chocolate ice cream and blend until smooth. Pour the mixture into glasses and decorate with grated chocolate.

Serving: Serve at once.

Chocolate shake

To be continued

Creamy Banana Shake

Ingredients :

- *1 - Very ripe Banana*
- *2 tsp – Castor sugar/powdered sugar*
- *1 cup – Cold milk*
- *2 small scoops – Vanilla ice cream*
- *Chocolate sprinklers*

Creamy banana shake

Preparation and Cooking:

- Chop banana and put into electric blender, add castor sugar and churn to smooth puree.
- Add the milk and one scoop of ice cream and blend again.
- Pour the mixture into a tall glass and place the second scoop of the ice cream.

Serving: Garnish with chocolate sprinklers; place a straw in it and serve at once.

Preparation time: 15 minutes.

Roasted Chicken Legs

Ingredients :

- *6 - Chicken legs*
- *1/4 cup – Vinegar*
- *1 tsp Ginger - Garlic paste each*
- *1 tsp - salt*
- *1/2 tsp - Red chili powder*
- *2 tbsp - Worcestershire sauce*
- *1 tbsp - Tomato puree*
- *1 tbsp - Cooking oil*

Preparation and Cooking:

- **Clean and wash** chicken legs. **Dry** them with a kitchen towel.
- With a **sharp knife** put some gashes (cut) on chicken legs. **Mix together** all the remaining ingredients in a bowl and **apply the mixture** on chicken legs properly. Place the legs in a bowl and cover. **Keep aside overnight under refrigeration.**
- Next day whenever you want to cook, **take the chicken out before 1 hour,** so that it reaches room temperature.
- **Place Chicken in a pan** with a lid and cook it covered on medium fire till the liquid evaporates. Switch off the fire.
- **Preheat the convection mode** of your OTG / Microwave oven at 180 degrees Celsius for 15 minutes.
- Meantime cover **the rack of your oven with aluminum foil** and place the chicken legs on that in a single layer. Whatever juices of chicken are left in the pan, **brush the chicken legs** with it.
- Now **roast them for 30 minutes.** In between turn the side of the

Roasted Chicken Legs

Important :
*This tasty and healthy **high protein Chicken dish** is the one for which you have to preplan and get the raw material such as chicken legs in advance, so that can be marinated for the best results*

To be continued

legs and keep roasting till done. (approximately for 15 to 20 minutes) **If needed, roast for another 10 minutes.**

- Remove the dish and **cover with foil** to keep it warm till used.

Roasted Chicken Legs

Serving:

Enjoy it when still warm with any salad, soup or as such sauce with green chutney.

***Health benefits of eating chicken*:**

Since ages chicken is being consumed as a food all over the world. Important part of poultry, chicken is one of the most popular meats eaten fondly in various forms. it is the good source of high protein, but low in fat and calories, is also very rich in numerous vitamins and minerals, that are important for making body mussels. Dieting on boiled, grilled or roasted chicken improves immune system and is ideal for weight loss. It controls blood pressure, reduces cholesterol and reduces cancer risk. Vitamins such as C, B6, A, E and K are also provided to the body. Breast of the chicken is considered the best white lean meat and mostly it is used for preparing Tandoori Tikkas and Soups containing boneless shredded meat.

Cooking time: 30 minute.

Italian Cookies

Ingredients :

- *2 and ½ cups - Flour*
- *Sugar - 1 tbsp*
- *1 tsp - Vanilla*
- *1 tsp - Lemon rind*
- *1/2 tsp – Salt*
- *4 - Eggs beaten*
- *Oil - For deep-frying*
- *1 cup - Honey*
- *Candy sprinklers for garnishing*

Italian Cookies

Preparation and Cooking:

- **Combine** sugar, lemon rind, vanilla and salt in a large bowl.
- **Add** eggs and half the flour; stir well; **mix** in the remaining flour and **make soft dough**. Knead well.
- **Divide the flour** into 20 to 24 pieces; with your hands **roll** each piece into a pencil shape. **Cut** each pencil into ½ -inch pieces.
- **Heat oil** and fry all the pieces in oil till **golden brown** and place in a large bowl.
- **Heat honey** to a boiling point; **pour over cookies and mix well.**
- With a **slotted spoon**, spoon the cookies on to a serving platter and slowly mound in a tree. Shape, (if you desire so.)

Serving:

Decorate the cookies with candy sprinklers. Cool them completely before serving.

Cooking time: 45 to 60 minutes.

***Famous** Italian cookies are prepared baked as well as fried. These cookies tossed in hot honey are unique in taste and look.*

Vanilla Custard Ice-cream

Ingredients :

- *2 and 1/2 cups - Full cream milk*
- *1/2 cup – Sugar*
- *1/4 cup – Butter*
- *1/4 cup - Corn flour*
- *3 - Egg yolks*
- *1/4 cup - Cream,*
- *1 tbsp - Vanilla essence*

Preparation and Cooking:

- **Place** eggs, sugar, corn flour and vanilla essence n a thick-bottomed pan and **beat with electric beater** until creamy.
- **Heat** milk and butter till the butter **melts. Pour** it over the beaten egg mixture slowly, **stirring constantly** and thoroughly. **Cook** the mixture over **boiling water** or use double-boiler, **constantly** beating till it starts thickening and **coating the back** of the spoon.Remove from the fire and cool.
- **Whip** the cream and **fold** into the custard.
- **Freeze** the mixture until firm, say after about 4 to 5 hours. Remove it from the freezing tray; **chop it roughly** and **beat** with the electric mixer **until smooth**.
- **Return** the ice-cream to the freezer tray once again and freeze until firm. You may **repeat** the process of **chopping** and **beating** it once more to get very **smooth consistency**.

Vanilla Custard Ice-cream

Home-made vanilla ice-cream *is very popular in parts of the country; though commercial ice creams are available in plenty under numerous popular brand names, but home-made has distinct taste and flavour. This recipe is for the basic ice cream and this becomes the base for so many different flavours.*

To be continued

Serving: Serve it as and when required.

Variation:

Make Chocolate Ice-cream:

Melt 150 gm of cooking chocolate and add to the vanilla ice-cream at Step-2 after cooking the custard. Rest, follow the same procedure.

Tips:

Ice cream can be prepared a couple of days in advance. Quantity can be doubled orincreased as per your requirement.

Cooking time: 30 minutes and freezing time extra.

Vanilla custard Ice-cream

Crunchy Cornflake Cookies

Crunchy Cornflake Cookies

Ingredients :

- *2 and 1/2 cup – Cornflakes*
- *1 cup – Flour*
- *1/2 cup – Butter*
- *1/3 cup – Sugar*
- *2/3 cup – Black raisins (sultanas),*
- *1 tsp – Baking powder,*
- *1 – Egg*

Preparation and Cooking:

- **Crush cornflakes** and **clean** raisins. **Powder** sugar.
- **Beat butter** and sugar with electric hand beater till light and fluffy.
- Break egg, beat it lightly and mix with sugar mixer.
- Sift flour and baking powder together twice and fold into the mixture. Add crushed cornflakes and raisins and mix lightly. Preheat your oven for moderate heat ie.180 degrees Celsius. Lightly grease a baking tray and keep aside.
- Divide the cookie mixture into equal sized portions. Lightly roll each portion on your palm and press it lightly. Finish rolling all the portions and place in the baking tray allowing room for spreading. Bake them in preheated oven for 20 minutes. Leave the tray in the oven for 5 minutes and then remove. Let the cookies cool.

Tips:

When completely cool, store them in an airtight container / cookie jar. This recipe will yield approximately 28 to 30 cookies.

Serving:

Serve them with any beverage at mid-day or tea time. They are ideal to be carried in your tiffin-box, too.

Cooking time: 20 minutes for preparation and 20 minutes baking.

Chocolate Coffee Mousse

Chocolate Coffee Mousse

Ingredients :

- *1 tin - Sweetened condensed milk*
- *1 tin - Hot water of equal measure*
- *3 tbsp - Coco powder*
- *1 tbsp - Coffee powder*
- *2 - Eggs*
- *4 tsp - Gelatin*
- *1/4 cup - Water to dissolve gelatin*
- *Pan of ice to fold soufflé on*
- *1 – Medium sized Jelly mould or small moulds*
- *Garnishing: ¼ to ½ cup fresh cream for garnishing (opt)*
- *Chocolate chips or chocolate sprinklers for garnishing (opt)*

Preparation and Cooking:

- **Clean jelly mould**; **brush** it with cooking oil, **rinse** with water without touching inside; **shake it** and **place it** in the deep freezer to chill.
- **Separate the** egg yolks and whites.
- Open the tin of condensed milk and **pour** it in a large bowl. **Mix** hot water, coco and coffee powder, and egg yolks. **Beat** thoroughly with electric rotary beater.
- **Mix gelatin with 1/4 cup of water** in a small bowl and **dissolve** it on the pan of hot water till it is **clear and transparent**, and now **pour** it into the milk and coco mixture. Beat it once again until

__What mousse is?__ The term '__Mousse__' is of French origin. Mousse means foam in French. It stands for soft food preparation. Mousse can be sweet as well as savoury. Sweet mousses are made with whipped egg whites that incorporate air bubble to give the dish light and fluffy texture. Sweet mousses are typically flavoured with chocolate, coffee, caramel, pureed fruits, vanilla and mint etc. Sometimes mousse is stabilized with gelatin. Mostly sweet mousses are served as a dessert and are chilled before serving. Savouries are flavoured with herbs and condiments.

To be continued

well blended. Now **cool** the mixture on pan of ice.

- **Put** enough water in a trove; **place** the mixture bowl in it to **take out the heat**; after a while **replac**e water with cold water and ice cubes. **Keep stirring the mixture** with a spatula to **avoid the lumps**. After about 10 minutes the mixture will start thickening.
- Meantime, **beat egg whites very stiff** and **fold** into the thickening mixture. Once it is thick **pour** it into the chilled mould.
- **Remove** the mould from the freezer and **pour** the mixture into it; **replace the** mould into the freezer once again for 35 to 40 minutes or till set. Later **cover** the mould with cling wrap and **place** it in the **cold part** of your refrigerator till in use.

Note:

Keep the covered soufflé in the deep freezer only if it is likely to be served next day or even later; but take it out at least 6 hours before use and store in the refrigerator.. Chilling the mould before-hand reduces the setting time.

Serving:

Run a palate or butter knife inside the mould carefully to loosen the soufflé and un-mould it onto a chilled plate. Cover it with cream and garnish with chocolate chips and serve. Cut the soufflé in wedges and serve in quarter plates.

Tips: *Cold soufflés for desserts are generally served un-mould, but if you set it in small glass bowls, you may serve individually without being un-mould.*

Cooking time: 30 minutes and chilling time extra.

Grilled Fish Kebabs

Grilled Fish Kebabs

Ingredients :

- *500 gm - Fresh thick fish fillets*
- *2 tbsp - Lemon juice*
- *1 tsp - Garlic paste*
- *1 tsp - Pepper powder*
- *1 large Green and Red pepper each*
- *2 tbsp - Olive / cooking oil*
- *A few leaves - Basil*
- *salt to taste and Chaat masala as per requirement*
- *10 to 12 - Metal / Bamboo skewers*

Preparation and Cooking:

- If using bamboo skewers, **soak them** in cold water.
- **Cut fish** in 1 and 1/2-inch squares; **marinate** with lemon juice, garlic, salt and pepper; and stand it for 30 minutes.
- Meantime, **cut the peppers also** in the same size. **Sprinkle** 1 tbsp oil, salt and pepper powder and keep aside.
- Now **arrange the fish and vegetables** alternately on the **skewers; brush lightly with oil** and place on grilling rack.
- **Preheat the grill** for 3 minutes. Grill the kebabs for 12minutes. After 7 minutes **turn** the side and continue cooking for another 5 minutes.

Serving: Remove the cooked kebab skewers and sprinkle a little Chaat masala over them. Serve in individual plates garnished with basil leaves.

Note: *Health benefits of Fish have already been written under the recipe Fish Cakes.*

Cooking time: 12 minutes.

Chicken and Semolina Pattice

Chicken Semolina Pattice

Ingredients :

- *3/4 cup – Semoling*
- *2 cups - Milk*
- *1 large - Boiled potato*
- *1/2 cup – Flour*
- *200 gm - Chicken mince (kheema)*
- *1 tsp - Ginger powder*
- *1 tsp - Dry oregano*
- *2 - Green chilies chopped*
- *1/4 cup – Coriander chopped (opt)*
- *Salt – n- pepper to taste*
- *Oil for frying*

Preparation and Cooking:

- **Place** semolina in a microwave safe medium bowl and **cook** for 2 minutes. Stir. **Add 2** tsp salt, 1 tsp pepper powder, oregano and milk. **Cook in** microwave for 3 minutes, uncovered. **Remove** the bowl wearing the gloves. Stir with a wooden spoon and **leave aside to cool.**
- Meantime **mince the kheema** in electric mincer. **Grate** boiled potato.
- **Mix** all the remaining ingredients, except oil, with semolina. **Transfer** the mixture in a trove. **Add** minced chicken meat and potato. **Mash the mixture** with your hand and **convert** into smooth dough, **divide** it into equal sized portions (of tennis bowl size).

Health Benefits: *This dish is a high protein diet with a little carbs too. The dish is like a meal along with a good salad or a soup. It is ideal even for those who like to avoid potato cutlets for various reasons. These are excellent for your lunch box. If you want to make them for your party, shape into small sized balls.*

To be continued

- **Smear your palms** with a little oil and **roll** the each portion. **Shape** the cutlets any way **you fancy** or use heart shaped Cookie-cutter; **fill it** up tightly and **taper** it lightly and **slide** the heart shaped cutlet. **Shape** all the balls in similar fashion.
- **Heat oil** to boiling point and **lower** the heat. **Line a plate** with kitchen paper. **Fry** the cutlets 1 or 2 at a time on medium high fire.
- **Remove** with a slotted spoon and **place** on the plate lined with **kitchen paper**.

Serving:

Serve them with grated carrot and finely chopped cabbage etc. Green Chutney / Tomato sauce is the best accompaniment. These cutlets can be served as a part of Continental meal.

Cooking time: 45 minutes to 1 hour.

Lassi/ Chhachh

For basic simple Lassi:

Ingredients :

- *1 cup – Curds*
- *4 cups - Water*
- *Salt –n- pepper to taste (opt)*

Preparation and Cooking:

- **Beat curds** in an electric mixer or by hand beater and mix it with drinking water. **Pour** in 4 glasses and **serve**. **Crushed** ice can be added in hot months. You may **enjoy it plain** along with meals or season it with seasonings.

Note: *Readymade Chhachh-masala is available and ½ tsp leveled can be added to each glass to enrich the taste.*

Popular Variations:

Mango Lassi

Ingredients :

Churn together ¼ cup – Mango pulp, ¼ cup- Curds and 1 tbsp – Sugar, add ½ cup cold water and blend., Pour in tall glass and serve or enjoy.

A pinch of ginger powder or mint powder can be added to enrich the taste.

Salty masala Lassi

Mango sweet Lassi

***Lassi** is one of the most important pro-biotic foods in Indian meals. This curd based beverage is integral part of the meals; from north to south it is consumed either with breakfast or with lunch very fondly and compulsorily. Its cooling effect nullifies the sharpness of chilies which are one of the ingredients of Indian dishes. It is the best accompaniment to a spicy meal. It also prevents dehydration.*

To be continued

Strawberry Lassi

Ingredients :

Churn together *¼ cup – Strawberry pulp, ¼ cup- Curds and 1 tbsp – Sugar, add ½ cup -cold water and blend.*
Pour in tall glass and serve or enjoy.
Fresh basil can be added to it.

Health Benefits of basic Lassi: Lassi/ Chhachh is not only a good source of protein but also of potassium, B vitamins, minerals and antioxidants. These nutrients boost immunity, improve sleep, enable hormone synthesis and much more. It also lowers cholesterol; reduces blood pressure and prevents cancer. In hot weather Lassi-a combination of water, yogurt, salt and spices replenish the body fluid and electrolyte levels instantly. It is a boon for the people who have lactose intolerance. Lactose intolerant people are actually able to digest yogurt without a problem, hence get proper calcium intake too.

Preparation time: 10 minutes.

Strawberry sweet lassi

Plain Lassi

Burritos

Burritos

__Burritos__ are Mexican flour tortillas, rolled with a filling inside and served warm. 'Burrito' is a popular Mexican dish prepared domestically and commercially and eaten very fondly all over Mexico and United State of America. They are prepared with flour or wheat-flour + refined flour together. Both the flours are kneaded together into pliable dough; rolled like big sized Indian Chapaties and cooked over griddle. According to taste Veg or non-veg filling can be stuffed and followed the process. These days flour tortillas are available in the super markets.

Ingredients :

- *6 large - Wheat tortillas (cooked in advance)*
- *3 cups - Veg or non-veg stuffing*
- *1 and 1/2 cup - Cooked white rice*
- *1 cup - Cheese grated*
- *1 cup - Pickled vegetable finely chopped/ chopped jalapeno*
- *2 cups - Tomato sauce/ red Mexican sauce or salsa*

Preparation and Cooking:

- Lightly oil a baking tray.
- **To assemble place** 1 tortilla on the working surface; **spread** 3 to 4 tbsp filling on it, 1-inch away from one end; sprinkle grated cheese generously over it; **sprinkle** 2 tbsp rice and **finally top** with 2 tbsp pickled vegetables or a few pieces of jalapeno.
- **Fold 1-inch inside** from the bottom; now fold the left end over it and roll forward to give a proper **cylindrical shape**. Fold all he burritos like this and place in the tray. **Now heat** in a preheated electric oven for **10 minutes** or till heated through **but not crisp.** Or you may heat them in a microwave but first cover them loosely with 2 layers of paper napkins and then heat on REHEAT mode for 2 minutes only.

To be continued

Note:

Take some adult's help when cooking the dish for making tortillas.

Serving:

Serve in individual plates, garnished with red sauce as a main meal with other accompaniments such as a soup or a beverag

Tips:

For making filling:

Heat 3 tbsp – Olive oil in a large pan and lightly fry 1-chopped onion 2 tbsp garlic, 1 –deseeded and chopped green chili together in it. Now add 3 cups boiled or mashed Kidney beans or cooked and shredded Chicken, ¼ cup – Tomato puree, 1 tbsp – Chili sauce, 3 tbsp chopped coriander /parsley, 1 tsp dry – Oregano and Salt to taste. Mix thoroughly and cool.

You may prepare filling with finely chopped mix vegetables and eggs too.

Cooking time: 35 to 45 minutes if tortillas are cooked before hand.

Ttrifle Pudding with Sponge Cake

Ttrifle Pudding with Sponge Cake

Ingredients :

For Sponge Cake

- *1 cup – Flour*
- *1cup – Sugar*
- *3 - Eggs*
- *2 tsp – Lemon juice*
- *1/3 cup-Milk*
- *1 tsp – Baking powder*
- *A pinch – Salt*
- *1 tbsp – Butter*

Preparation and Baking:

- **Preheat** Convection mode of your electric oven/ microwave oven or cooking range at **180 degrees Celsius.**
- **Sift** flour, salt and baking powder together.
- **Beat eggs** with a rotary beater until light and foamy. Beating constantly, gradually add sugar, lemon juice and flour mixture.
- Heat milk and butter for 30 seconds and add to beaten eggs, stir until smooth.
- Pour into a 9-inch un-greased baking tin. Bake in a moderately hot oven for 40 to 45 minutes.
- Remove the cake from oven and invert on cooling wire rack. Leave it foe 30 minutes at least. Un-mould the cake.
- **Usage:** Use the sponge cake for trifle pudding or put icing over it for birthday cake etc.

__'Trifle pudding'__ means a pudding in three layers. For your knowledge, I must explain that in common practice we place __1st layer__ of any plain cake, __2nd layer__ of thin custard/ chocolate sauce/fresh cream and __3rd layer__ of fresh fruits/dry fruits or jelly cubes etc. Then you may garnish in your own style. In the following recipe we will be substituting custard with Vanilla ice cream and using fresh colourful fruits as the top layer. Our base will be __Hot milk sponge cake that contains minimum fat, hence, is used for trifles and icing.__

Plan and get the essential ingredients in advance before preparing this dish.

To be continued

For trifle you need:

- *1 - sponge cake*
- *I family sized slab of Vanilla ice-cream*
- *1/2 cup – sweet lemon water*
- *A few fresh seasonal fruits or 8 to 10 - Strawberries*
- *2 –Kiwi fruits*
- *2 slices of preserved – Pineapple*
- *1 small – Apple*
- *A few Orange segments and some sprinklers*

Assembling:

- **Slice all** the fruits thinly. **Slice apple** without peeling it.
- **Slice the cake** from the center; **spread both the pieces** separately on working surface; and **sprinkle lemon** water on them to soak the cake.
- **Apply thick layer** of vanilla ice cream with the aid of **butter knife**; spread; if you like **place single layer** of sliced fruits on one layer of the cake; and **cover it** with the other half of the cake.
- Place the cake in a shallow dish or on a platter. **Soak the** top also with a little **lemon water**. **Apply** quickly a thick layer of **ice cream** on top of the cake and place it under refrigeration for 30 minutes.
- **Remove and decorate** it with fresh fruit and sprinklers etc. You may **sprinkle** lightly the toasted and crushed **dry fruits** such as almond, cashew or pistachio nuts.

Tips: *You can buy sponge cake if you have to prepare the dish in a hurry.*

To vary: Mix fruits and jelly cubes for top layer. For this set jelly before hand; Dissolve jelly crystals with ½ cup less water recommended on the packet.

Cooking time: Depends upon you, whether you are baking a sponge cake or buying it.

Lava Cakes

Lava Cakes

Ingredients :

- *100 gm - Dark chocolate compound broken into pieces or chocolate chips*
- *100 gm - butter*
- *1 cup - Powdered/icing sugar*
- *3 - Large eggs*
- *1/2 cup – Sieved flour*
- *1/2 tsp – Vanilla essence*

Preparation and Bakin:

- **Prepare** 4 ramekins or about 6 to 8 paper cups by **greasing** them well with **butter**, or spraying them well with salt
- **Preheat** your electric oven/ convection mode of a microwave/cooking range to **200 degrees Celsius.**
- **Combine** chocolate compound and butter together in a medium sized micro-safe bowl and **melt** in a microwave **for 1 minute** and stir; after that each time run your microwave **for 30 seconds** and stir till the chocolate is fully melt. **Or** melt the chocolate and butter **over pan of hot water.** Here take help of a grown up.
- **Mix together** eggs and sugar and beat till well blended. Add flour and vanilla essence. Now pour the melted chocolate mixture in it and **beat** till well mixed.
- **Place** the paper cups/ ramekins in a baking tray and **bake** in the hot oven for **12 minutes**. Remove the tray (wearing gloves).

Lava cakes *are warm, gooey chocolate dessert which has stolen the hearts of children all over, and the chocolate lovers who want to give themselves a special treat. Lava molten cakes are made of dark chocolate and that is considered good for heart and blood circulation. They say that dark chocolate reduces the risk of heart stroke. Anyway, treat yourself with this wonderful chocolate molten dessert but with a limit, as* ***'moderation'*** *is always the key word for good health.*

To be continued

- ***Note:*** *Do not pay much attention to the top of the cakes.*

Serving: This dessert is served hot, so **run a butter knife** inside the ramekin or a paper cup and **invert the cake** in a serving plate. The centre of the cake should be **moist** when served, so that when someone eats **lava should flow.**

Baking time: 12 minutes.

Lava cake with a beverage

Grilled Open Sandwich

Grilled Open Sandwich

Ingredients :

- *1 - French bread*
- *1/4 cup – Tomato sauce*
- *1 tsp - Chili-garlic sauce*
- *1 tsp - Oregano (dry)*
- *1/2 cup – Mozzarella cheese sliced.*

Preparation and Cooking:

- **Cut bread diagonally.** Mix together tomato sauce and chili garlic and spread on the diagonally sliced bread.
- **Cover** the bread with **sliced mozzarella** cheese and **sprinkle** a little oregano on top.
- Arrange the bread on grilling rack **and grill each lot for 6 to 7 minutes in pre-heated grill.**
- **Enjoy** the grilled sandwiches hot / warm with or without any beverage.

Always Preheat Grill or Oven before Grilling or Baking.

Healthy Moong Sprouts Chaat

Ingredients :

- *2 cups - Washed Moong sprouts*
- *1/4 cup-chopped Onions (opt)*
- *1/2 cup- chopped Tomatoes*
- *1 - tsp - Chaat masala*
- *Salt-n-Pepper to taste*
- *1 - Lemon*
- *2 tbsp - Coriander (opt)*
- *1 tsp - Cooking oil*

Moong Sprouts Chaat

Preparation and Cooking:

- **Place sprouts** in a micro-safe bowl, **cover and cook** for 2 minutes in a micro oven.

  Or **place** sprouts, 1 tsp oil and 1/4 cup water in a pan; **cover and cook** for 4 minutes; remove and cool.
- **Squeeze** the lemon over moong. **Add** rest of the ingredients and **check** the seasonings.
- **Adjust** salt and pepper if required.
- Eat it as a snack whenever you are hungry.

For Making Moong Sprouts -

Soak ½ cup whole Moong for 6-8 hours drain the water and place moong in if colander(Chalni).Cover and keep at warm place for 36 hours. (In-between after 24 hours sprinkle a little water over moong, toss and cover. Keep for another 12 hours.)

Remove from colander and store under refrigeration.

Roasted Crunchy Bread Croutons Salad

Roasted Bread Croutons Salad

Ingredients :

- *1 to 1 and 1/4 cup - Roasted croutons*
- *1-Large chopped tomato*
- *2- Spring onions chopped along with their tender greens*
- *1 medium – Cucumber chopped*
- *1/4 cup – French dressing*
- *Salt-n-Pepper to taste*
- *A few salad leaves*

Preparation and Cooking:

- **Wash** salad leaves and **soak in cold water** for 15 to 30 minutes; **remove** and shake them well; now **break them** in edible sized pieces and **refrigerate** till used; **cover** and **place** under refrigeration for 20 to 30 minutes.
- In a bowl **mix all** the chopped ingredients and **place** them to under refrigeration.
- Just before serving **mix together** chopped salad leaves, croutons and chopped vegetables and pour French dressing over the ingredients. **Toss** the salad well and enjoy it cold.

Note: You can also roast Fox nuts

Place 1 cup plain nuts in a bowl; brush them with a little cooking oil and sprinkle a little table salt; mix and micro cook for **2 minutes** in a microwave oven. Cool and use. Eat them like a healthy crunchy snack.

For French dressing:

Mix together in a bottle, ¼ cup – Table vinegar, ¼ cup –Olive / vegetable oil, 1tsp –Dry mustard powder, 1 tsp – Sugar, ¼ tsp - Pepper powder and Salt to taste. Shake the bottle well and refrigerate till in use. Always shake it again before pouring in any salad.

Savoury Biscuits Topped with Cheese and Veggies

Ingredients :

- *Any Salted Biscuits / cheese crackers*
- *Cheese spread*
- *Cheese slices*
- *Cucumber*
- *Tomatoes*

Preparation :

- **Cut tomato and cucumber in thin slices**. Cut cheese slices into 4 pieces each
- **Place biscuits** on chopping board; **spread cheese** with a butter knife on biscuits. **Place 1 piece** cheese on each biscuit; **dot it** with a little sauce and **top with** a slice of cucumber and a piece of cherry tomato.
- Serve / eat within 15 minutes before biscuits lose their crispness.

Variation:

If you prefer, you may use mustard sauce, mayonnaise or chili sauce instead of cheese spread.

Cheese Crackers

Salted Biscuits

Roasted Berries

Roasted Berries

Ingredients :

- *1tsp - Olive-oil*
- *1/2 cup - Blue berries*
- *12 - Small strawberries*
- *2 tbsp - Powdered sugar*
- *12 to 16 - Raspberries (golden-berries)*

Information :

All the **berries**, including strawberries, raspberries, blue berries and even gooseberries, as well as all the **variety of edible berries** are valuable nutritional foods with great cleansing properties. They all contain a high percentage of water ranging from 80 to 90 percent. All the **berries** are rich in **potassium** and other **mineral elements;** and when ripe, c**ontain valuable natural sugars** which contain in cleansing the system. So **must be eaten** in one or other way. This simple seasonal dish is very delicious for the berries' lovers.

Preparation and Cooking:

- **Clean** all the berries and **remove** the stems and leaves etc.
- **Heat up** one nonstick pan and **apply olive oil** with a brush.
- **Add all** the berries and **roast** them for 5 minutes. **Remove** from fire and **sprinkle** powdered sugar all over the berries
- **Serve them warm** as a fruit starter/ dessert or **enjoy them** just a fun fruits mixture to satiate your hunger.

Note: Powdered sugar will reduce the sour taste of berries and enhance the sweetness.
It will take about 10 minutes.

Mixed Melons

Mixed Melons

Ingredients :

- *1 small - Water melon*
- *1 - fruitball scooper*
- *1 large - Melon green from inside(honeydew)*
- *1 large - Melon orange from inside (cantaloupe)*
- *A few tooth picks or small fruit forks*

Information :

Orange melons are a great source of Vitamin A and Vitamin C in the form of carotenoids. It also provides potassium and B vitamins, including thiamine, niacin and vitamin K, magnesium and fiber.

Green melons are also rich n fiber that can aid in food digestion. Vitamin C in honeydew melons helps boost body's immune system to fight off bacteria and illness.

Watermelon juicy and refreshing fruit is full of nutrients. It contains Vitamins A , B6 and C, antioxidants and amino acids. It is fat free and very low in sodium.

Preparation :

Cut the melons into halves and **remove** the seeds. Take out **as many balls as** you can with the h**elp of fruit ball scooper**. Same way **cut** the water melon and scoop out as many balls as possible.

You will take about 30 to 40 minutes.

Arrange : The balls in a layer in a shallow dish and serve along with fruit forks/ toothpicks.

Tips: *After taking out balls, scrape the water melon/ melons and pass through a liquidizer with some ice cubes and powdered sugar. Pour in juice glasses and garnish with 1 or 2 balls and mint leaves if you like.*

Cheese Cream Dip

Cheese Cream Dip

Ingredients :

- *2 cups - Fresh curds*
- *1 tsp - Salt*
- *1/4 tsp - Black pepper*
- *2 tsp - Sugar*
- *1 - tsp - Olive oil/ cooking oil*
- *Juice from 1/2 - Lemon*
- *1tbsp - Finely chopped coriander/ mint or 1 tsp - chopped parsley*
- *1 - white clean kitchen duster or muslin cloth*
- *1 - Strainer*

Preparation :

How to make hung curd for cheese cream?

Place strainer on a deep bowl / vessel. **Soak the kitchen napkin/** muslin cloth and **squeeze** it properly; **spread** it over strainer and **put** the curds in it; **cover** and **leave** it aside for2 hours. After 2 hours you will find thick curds in the strainer; **remove** it with a spoon and **keep** under **refrigeration**. Now this is your **'hung curd'.**

For preparing dip, **Add rest** of the ingredients except green coriander etc, and **beat** properly. Now **add** fresh coriander/ mint, mix and **keep** under refrigeration till used.

Serving : You can serve the fresh vegetables sticks of Carrot and Cucumber, any Chips, Cheese straws or Soup-sticks etc along with it.

Tips:
Hung curd is also used to make salads or to marinate Chicken pieces and boiled baby Potatoes to make tandoori Tikkas and tandoori Aaloo respectively.

Plain Mini Idlis

One of the popular pro-biotic foods

Plain Idli

Ingredients :

- *500 gm- Basic Idli Batter*
- *1 tbsp - Cooking oil*
- *1 tsp - Salt*
- *Small idli moulds along with its vessel*

Preparation and Cooking:

- **Keep the basic idli batter** at least for **12 hours** out of refrigerator , or till it is well **fermented**. Add salt and mix well.
- With a brush **oil the mini idli moulds**. **Add 1 cup** water in the vessel and **place** on fire.
- Meantime **put 1 spoon batter** in each **cavity** of idlimould, Now **stack** the moulds in idli vessel or pressure cooker, **close the lid** and **increase** the fire to full.

- **Cook for** 3 minutes on full fire and switch off the fire. **Remove** the vessel; **open** the lid and take out idlimoulds. Let the idlis **cool** and then **remove** with a butter knife or a palate knife.
- **Enjoy** with Coconut chutney. Or **tamper idlis** with **mustard seeds** and **curry leaves** in 2 tbsp hot oil.

Tips :

*You can make masala idli with 'ready to cook' mixture mixed with beaten curds (as per instructions on the packet). Let the mixture stand for 15 to 20 minutes and then follow the procedure to steam the idlis as mentioned in the recipe of 'Plain idli' With Basic **idli-batter**, you can also cook Mini Uttapams and Appas.*

Mini Uttapams

Ingredients :

- *Basic idli batter - 500 gm*
- *1 large - Tomato chopped*
- *2 tbsp - Coriander chopped*
- *1 to 2 - Green chili chopped fine*
- *2 tbsp - Cooking oil*
- *Salt to taste*
- *A large pinch - Asafetida(opt)*
- *Mini Uttapam Pan*

Plain Uttapam

Preparation and Cooking:

- **Mix all** the chopped ingredients **into basic idli batter.**
- **Brush the cavities** of Mini uttapams' pan and **place** it on fire. **Heat** the pan and lower the heat.
- Now **put 1 tbsp mixed batter** in each cavity of utapam pan and **sprinkle** a little **oil** over the uttapams. **Cook** on medium fire. After about 3**0 seconds change** the side of uttapams with palate knife and cook again till golden brown.
- **Remove** them and **store** in a hot case lined with four f**old kitchen napkin**. Repeat the process with the remaining batter.
- Enjoy them with Coconut chutney and Red onion-tomato chutney.

Spinach Uttapam

Tips:

*For making Appas, the same idli batter is used; you can add grated carrot, grated fresh coconut, finely chopped butter beans or capsicums etc along with salt, pepper and a little asafetida. Then cook them in preheated and greased **Appa-Patar** on medium fire. Just put 1 tbsp prepared batter in each cavity; cover for a few seconds; uncover; brush them with a little oil and turn their side with the help of a butter knife or a stick provided along the vessel; cover again and cook till Appas are golden brown.*

Remove and serve / enjoy with any chutney.

Fruit Salad

Mix Fruit Salad

Ingredients :

- *1 - medium - Apple*
- *1 - Pear*
- *1 - Orange*
- *A few Strawberries*
- *1/2 cup - Grapes*
- *1 - Lemon*
- *Salt -n- pepper or lemon pepper*

Preparation and Cooking:

- Fruits are an important part of our life, as they are full of vitamins and minerals they improve our health and help us to maintain our immunity and digestion etc. Though most of the fruits are full of Vitamin C, yet each fruit has different contents and even the quantity varies. For example, all the Berries and Citrus fruit have good quantity of Vitamin C in them. Fruits like Apple Orange, Lemon, Mango, Grapes, Papaya and Apricot etc give us Vitamin A and Vitamin B. Papaya also gives Vitamin D. Vitamin B is also found in Pear and Figs etc. Mixed fruits impart the minerals and vitamins both, hence mixed fruit salad.
- Wash clean & cut the Fruits.

Tips:
Dry fruits, such as Almonds, Cashew or Walnuts can also be added to the fruit salad, but dry fruits should be soaked for 4 to 6 hours. Then they are revived and are easier to digest. Adding dry fruits enhances the taste and its value.

Note : You can mix fruits according to the season, For example, Mango, Pomegranate, Papaya, Melons, Tomatoes and Dragon Fruit etc can be mixed with other available fruits.Wash, clean and cut fruits either in cubes or in segment style. Squeeze lemon over fruits to avoid de-colouration. Place them in a bowl, cover and keep under refrigeration at-least for 30 minutes. Sprinkle salt and pepper / lemon pepper over fruits and serve. You can eat fruit salad without cooling too.You can use fruit forks /forks /toothpicks to enjoy fruit salad.

Hot Chocolate

Ingredients :

- *500 ml - Milk / skimmed milk*
- *100 gm - Plain dark chocolate*
- *1 tbsp - Powdered sugar (opt)*
- *A small pinch Cinnamon powder (opt)*

Preparation and Cooking:

- One of the **most popular drinks** amongst children like you is the Hot Chocolate; and here we are giving you a very easy and popular recipe to prepare it
- **Chop the chocolate** into small pieces and **place** in a deep pan; **pour 1** cup milk or water and **melt** the chocolate on medium fire. **Bring** the mixture to the **boiling point** and remove from fire.
- **Heat** the remaining milk on low fire. Meantime with a whisk or electric rotary beater **beat the chocolate mixture** until the chocolate is completely melted and the mixture is thick and foamy.
- Gradually, **pour the remaining hot milk** and whisk again. **Warm** over low heat and s**erve or enjoy**.

Hot Chocolate

Health Benefits

You all know that coco / cocoa - main ingredient of chocolate was discovered in Mexico, later Spanish introduced it into Europe. In spite of their fat contents Cocoa beans are rather nutritious. They supply useful amounts of Proteins, some B vitamins and trace elements of iron and magnesium. Chocolate preparations give instant boost of energy because of its sugar content, hence, should be consumed in moderation.

Lemonade

Ingredients :

- *1/2 cup - Sugar*
- *3/4 cup - Fresh Lime juice (approximately from 6 - Sweet limes)*
- *4 cups - Drinking water*
- *1/2 cup - Ice cubes*
- *4 - Tall glasses*

Preparation :

Add sugar and lime juice in electric mixture and **churn** properly. **Add** 1 cup water and **churn** again. Now add remaining water and **check** the sweetness. **Place** 3 to 4 ice cubes in each glass and **pour** lemonade over ice.

You may decorate the glass with a slice of Lemon or Lime.

Serving :

Serve it immediately or sip it slowly to enjoy the refreshing coolness.

Nimbu-pani

Lemonade

***Lemonade** is one of the most popular-non-alcoholic drinks of Mexico. A glass of cold sweet-n-sour lemonade is one of their national drinks. This refreshing drink compliments Mexican meals (as they are tastefully spicy). Anyway, here we are giving you an easy to make recipe at home. It is as easy as Indian **Nimbu-pani** is. This refreshing drink is full of Vitamin C, so it is ideal for hot summers.*

Crepes

Crepes stage - 1

Ingredients :

- *1 cup - Flour*
- *1 - Egg*
- *1 spoon - cooking oil*
- *A pinch of salt.*
- *1 cup - Milk at room temperature*

Preparation and Cooking:

- **Sieve** the flour and salt in a bowl. **Make** a well in the centre; **break egg** and **beat** it first and then **pour** in the centre of the well in the flour. Slowly **pour** the milk; **add** oil and **beat** the batter till **smooth** and of pouring quality.

- **Heat** a medium sized non-stick pan with a handle; **lower** the fire; **brush** the pan with cooking oil; **pour** 1 ladle full of batter in the centre of pan and **tilt** it to spread the batter properly. **Cook** it from both sides on slow fire, giving each side at least ½ **minute. Remove** it with a flat spoon and place on aluminum-foil. **Repeat** the process with remaining batter and **enjoy** it with honey, maple syrup or jam etc.

Note:

If anyway batter seems thick add a few drops of more milk and beat once again.

Let the batter stand for 30 minutes.

***Crepes** are thin pancakes like discs. They can be eaten with honey, any jam or fruit sauce. They can be filled with ice cream and served with fruit sauce and fresh cream.*

To be continued

Variation 1:

Spread the crepe on a working board; **place** 1 tbsp **Vanilla ice-cream** in the centre and roll the crepe in a cylindrical fashion. This way **fill and roll** the other crepes and **chill** for 1hour. Meantime **make** Strawberry sauce or Chocolate sauce and pour over filled crepes and chill for 30 minutes

Filled Crepes Stage - 2

Strawberry sauce:

Mix together ½ cup Strawberry crush, ¼ cup Fresh cream and 2 tbsp Sugar in a bowl and beat.

Chocolate sauce:

Mix together 1 tbsp full Coco powder, 2 tbsp full Sugar and ½ cup Water. Cook the mixture on medium fire till the sauce is shining and of pouring consistency. Store in a clean and dry container under refrigeration you can also use ready This will last for 10 to 15 days.

Chocolate Sauce Crepes Stage - 3

You can also use ready-made sauce.

Variation 2 :

Fill the Crepes with finely chopped sauted mixed vegetables; roll them and stick with 1 toothpick each; brush with oil and bake them as Spring rolls for 5 minutes in hot oven. Remove and cut them.

Instant Tomato Soup

Tomato Soup

Ingredients :

- *1 - Pack Instant Tomato soup*
- *3 cups - Water*
- *2 tsp - fresh cream (opt)*
- *Some bread croutons or roasted Fox nuts (phool Makhana) or Soup sticks*

Preparation and Cooking:

- In a medium sized pan **add 3 cups water**. Cut **the packet** and add the contents to measured water.
- With an egg beater **mix the** contents (water and tomato powder) thoroughly.
- Now **place** the pan on fire and **let** the mixture reach the boiling **point.** Keep stirring with a wooden spoon to **avoid lumps.** Reduce the fire and **simmer** the soup for **10** minutes.
- **Remove** from fire and **pour** the soup in soup bowls or cups with a ladle.

Serving:

Garnish the soup cups with ½ tsp cream and roasted fox nuts / bread croutons or even Soup sticks/ Melba toast. Enjoy it hot or at room temperature.

It takes about 15 minutes.

Tips:

This way you can make any instant soup for yourself or loved ones, anytime and anywhere.

Baked Jacket Potato

Baked Jacket Potato

Ingredients :

- *6 - Large potatoes*
- *1 tbsp - Cooking oil*
- *1 cup - Coleslaw salad*

Preparation and Cooking:

- **Wash** the potatoes and **steam** them **unpeeled** in a microwave basket, in a micro oven for 6-minutes, **covered.**
- **Remove** from oven. **Brush a baking pan** with a little oil and **place** the potatoes in it.
- **Preheat your over** at 200 degrees Celsius for 5 minutes and **bake** potatoes in it for 1 hour at 200 degrees Celsius.
- After 30 minutes, **open the oven** (wearing the gloves) and **turn** the side of potatoes with a pair of tongs. **Close** the oven and **continue** baking the potatoes for another **30 minutes**.
- Wear the gloves and remove the pan from oven. Squeeze the potatoes with hand in glove; if it is pressed nicely, that means the potatoes are done. Place them in a plate and m**ark a cross** across the potatoes when **still warm**.
- **Fill the** potatoes with **cold Coleslaw** with the help of a spoon and a butter knife.

Note:

For Coleslaw: *Mix together 1 cup finely shredded white cabbage, 1small - Carrot grated, 1small - Apple grated sprinkled with 1 tbsp Lemon juice, 2 tbsp – Mayonnaise sauce, Salt-n-Pepper to taste (if needed). Chill the salad till used.*

Serving: Serve 1- potato each, when still warm, individually along with a fork and knife.

Chili Butter Crispies

Chili Butter Crispies

Ingredients :

- *1 - cup Flour*
- *½ cup - Wheat flour*
- *100 gm - Butter*
- *1 tbsp - Green chili paste*
- *¼ tsp - Dry oregano*
- *½ tsp - Salt*
- *2 tbsp - Curds*
- *1 tbsp - Lemon juice*

Preparation and Cooking:

- **Sift together flour,** wheat flour and salt together. **Sprinkle** oregano. **Add** chili paste. **Rub** in butter till the mixture resembles bread crumbs. **Add curds** and lemon juice; now **mix** to a soft dough and **gather the mixture** into a ball. **Wrap** it in a greaseproof paper and **refrigerate** for 1 hour.
- Take out the **chilled mixture and roll it** on clean surface and **roll** to a thin sheet (if by chance it sticks to surface while rolling, sprinkle the rolling space with a scanty layer of flour).
- **Cut** into desired shape with a **cookie cutter** and place in a **baking tray**. Preheat your oven for 5 minutes for moderate heat i.e. 180 degrees Celsius. **Bake** the biscuits for **15** minutes. **Remove** the tray and let the biscuits **cool** completely. **Remove** with your palate knife.

Note: Place the tray on the lower rack of your electric ovens, but if you are using a cooking range to bake, then place the tray on upper rack

Variation: *If you do not eat green chilies, you may add ¼ tsp chili powder and a few chili flakes.*

Serving : *Serve them at room temperature with any beverage or try them with Vanilla ice cream.*

Cooking time will be 15 minutes baking.

Kadah Prashad/ Hulwa/ Sheera

Ingredients :

- *1/2 cup - Semolina/Suji/Rawa*
- *1/4 cup - Wheat flour/Atta*
- *1/2 cup - Ghee/Clarified butter*
- *1 cup - Sugar*
- *2 and 1/2 cup - Water*

Preparation and Cooking:

- **Put** sugar and water in a deep **microwave bowl** and **cook** for 5 minutes. **Remove** the bowl and stir to dissolve sugar fully well.
- **Place** semolina in a micro-safe bowl and **cook** in microwave for **2** minute. **Open** the door and **stir** semolina; **add** wheat flour; and **cook** for **2** minutes more.
- **Take** a deep micro safe bowl with a lid, **put ghee** in it and **heat** it in micro oven for 1 minute. **Add roasted semolina** mixture and stir properly with a wooden spoon, and **cook for 4 minutes**, uncovered, stirring in between after 2 minutes.
- Remove the bowl (wearing gloves); **stir** the mixture; **wait** for a minute and pour sugar syrup in ghee mixture. Stir properly till the mixture is **lump** free. **Cover** the dish with a **lid** and cook in the microwave for 5 minutes; in between **stir after 3 minutes**. Cover and **continue** cooking for remaining 2 minutes.
- Let the dish **stand for 2minutes**. Mix the Hulwa **with a fork** and use as required. **It will take about 12 minute altogether.**

Serving: If Hulwa is to be eaten with puries, enrich it with nuts and raisins in the end when the dish is still hot.

Kadah Prashad/ Hulwa/ Sheera

***This dish** is a popular and nutritious Indian sweet that is consumed all over India in one or the other form. Mostly it is prepared as a PRASAD on all auspicious occasions for worshipping God in various forms. Simple Prasad offered to the gods is always prepared without any nuts, flavourings and condiments. When it is relished as a dessert or eaten with puries, then almond slivers, raisins, chopped cashew nuts, cardamom powder etc are added to enrich the taste. Here, simple recipe is being written for Prasad cooked in a microwave oven. Some people even add edible yellow colour too in it.*

Take help of a grown up person.

Wholemeal Biscuits

Ingredients :

- *150 gm – Butter*
- *1/4 cup – Sugar*
- *3/4 cup – Whole-meal flour*
- *3/4 cup – plain flour*
- *1/4 cup – Oats*

Preparation and Cooking:

- **Keep butter** at room temperature. **Powder** measured sugar. Powder measured oats.
- **Combine** butter and sugar in a bowl and **beat** with electric beater until mixture is **light and fluffy**.
- **Sift** whole-wheat flour and plain flour together and add powdered oats. **Mix well** with butter mixture.
- **Turn out** on **lightly floured surface**, and knead until **smooth**. Roll out to **1/2 -inch** thickness. **Cut** into any shape using a cookie cutter.
- Lightly grease a baking tray and place the biscuits in it. **Mark** them lightly. **Bake** them in moderately slow oven ie. 160 degrees Celsius for **30 minutes** or until lightly browned. Leave in oven for 10 minutes.
- **Remove** from oven and **leave to cool** in a tray on the platform.

Serving:

Serve with your choicest beverage or enjoy with your siblings/friends.

Wholemeal Biscuits

Butter Corn Cups

Ingredients :

- *300 gm - Sweet corn kernels*
- *2 tbsp - Butter*
- *1 and 1/4 tsp - Salt*
- *1/4 tsp - Black pepper powder*
- *Chat Masala to taste*
- *2 tbsp - Lemon juice*
- *2 tbsp - Coriander chopped (opt).*

Preparation and Cooking:

- **Wash corn kernels** and place them in micro safe bowl; **cover** and **steam** for 5 minutes. Stand the dish for 2 minutes.
- **Take the bowl out** and mix **butter**; stir it well with **rubber spatula** and **season it** with remaining ingredients **except coriander**.
- **Divide** the corn into 6 cups and **garnish** with chopped **coriander**.

Serving :

Serve the corn when still warm.

- **Cooking time : 15 minutes.**

Butter Corn Cups

About Corn :

Corn is considered good for the heart, skin and growing hair. it is good for heart muscles; stimulates brain action and digestion; reduces fatigue; increases stamina; prevents constipation; helps to maintain the normal red blood count and improves circulation; and promotes healthy skin.

Sandwiches

Ingredients :

- *16 slices - White/brown bread*
- *Butter*
- *Cheese spread*
- *Green chutney*
- *Cheese slices*

Or ham Slamies

- *Thinly sliced Tomatoes*
- *Cucumber*
- *Boiled potatoes and lettuce etc.*

Preparation and Cooking:

- **Apply butter** or cheese spread on slices; **place** the pieces of your favourite vegetables or cheese slices or meat slices on half the slices of bread; **place other half** pieces of bread on top and **press** a little with your **hand**, so that both the pieces of bread stick with each other.
- Now **with a sharp knife** you may **remove the brown sides** of the bread and **cut** from the center, either straight or diagonally, so that they can be handled better.
- **Cover the sandwiches** with a moist napkin till eaten, so that sandwiches don't get **dry.**

Note: If children you want to make round shaped sandwiches, cut them first with cookie cutter and then apply butter etc., otherwise plain sandwich with butter can be cut later

Tips: *For making **Chutney sandwiches**, apply thick chutney on half the slices and butter/cheese spread on the remaining slices.*

*For making **Jam sandwiches**, apply jam generously on half slices and butter/ cheese paste/ homemade Malai on the other half.*

Sandwiches

***Sandwich** is that food item which is prepared with two slices of any bread with a filling between them. Generally, bread slices are either buttered or some other sauce / paste is applied on them, and finally are filled with slices of vegetables, cheese and meat etc. Mostly, they are consumed after removing the sides, but these days many people like them grilled. Sandwiches are eaten as a light meal. They can be salty or sweet (Prepared with fruit jams, butter and sugar, Chocolate paste etc).*

Take help of a grown up person to get the vegetables sliced.

A Closing Word

With joy and gratitude I end this book. While developing recipes and writing their benefits for you dear children, I personally enjoyed it thoroughly. I hope that you will enjoy experimenting with recipes and will take keen interest in creating your favourite dishes. In the present time of popular apps like SWIGGY (which can procure your favourite dishes within no time) cooking your selected dish yourself in your free time will not only be a good change but also a lot of fun. I trust all of you that you will approach the task with a positive mind and will come out with flying colours, I mean will not go wrong in your attempts. Always expect the best. I will keep my fingers crossed for all of you.

Feedback is most welcome

Fun movements with children at workshop

Little food connoisseurs

About The Author

Prabhjot Mundhir, the writer is known for her research-oriented work and expertise in culinary arts. Her delicious recipes are not only authentic and innovative but also aesthetically presented. Her widely acclaimed books are ***Nutritious Mushroom, Paneer Bonanza, Corn Cuisine, Microwave Cooking - made easy, Microwave Cooking and Exotic Mexican Cuisine. 30 Day Rapidex Cookery Course*** (a practical course specially designed and created for beginners by self-learning) has been edited and illustrated by her. She also added the recipe section to the book.

Her book ***Microwave Cooking*** known for exclusive dishes cooked in a microwave is judged **The Best in India** (in Easy Recipe Category) by **Gourmand World Cookbook Awards** in 2011 and her ***Exotic Mexican Cuisine*** is judged the **Best Latin American Cuisine** in India by **Gourmand World Cookbook Awards** in 2012. Her ***Authentic Italian Cuisine*** was published in 2016.

Weekend Cookery - for boys and girls

As the name suggests, Weekend Cookery- for boys and girls, contains 52 main recipes and 20 recipes for the quick bites. Beside easy to cook –step by step recipes that are certainly good to eat, the book is packed with fascinating facts on the origin / development of the dishes; health benefits of the ingredients used in the recipes and tips on their variations. There is information on Chef's tools, cooking terminology and glossary of ingredients and their Hindi to English names. I am dead sure that children will not only have the fun while trying them but also enjoy enthusiastically sharing the information with the peer groups/dear ones.

During the cookery workshop sessions with growing up children, I was inspired to develop this book for our little chefs, so that they learn to appreciate what they are eating, why their parents insist on what to eat or what not to eat and how much labour of love is involved in creating their choicest delicious food. They will also learn the charm of self involvement in art of cooking to satiate their taste buds. I am sure that in this era of fast food this inspirational cookbook along with treating their taste buds with mouth watering dishes, will also make children appreciate the goodness of fresh home cooked food. Moreover, the tradition of cooking food with own hands and sharing with the dear ones creates a loving and strong bond between the plate and people (friends or family members). It is an interesting proven fact that the food is a great connect and reinforces family bonds.

PUBLISHER

UNICORN BOOKS PVT. LTD.
F-2/16, Ansari Road, Daryaganj, New Delhi - 110002

Ph.: 011-23262683, 23275434

Email: info@unicornbooks.in

Edition: 2019

ISBN: 978-81-7806-404-8

₹500.00
ISBN: 978-81-7806-404-8
9 788178 064048

UNICORNBOOKS
www.unicornbooks.in • info@unicornbooks.in